SAVING ENDANGERED SPECIES

THE
WHOOPING CRANE
Help Save This Endangered Species!

Alison Imbriaco

MyReportLinks.com Books
an imprint of

Enslow Publishers, Inc. **E**
Box 398, 40 Industrial Road
Berkeley Heights, NJ 07922
USA

MyReportLinks.com Books, an imprint of Enslow Publishers, Inc. MyReportLinks®
is a registered trademark of Enslow Publishers, Inc.

Library of Congress Cataloging-in-Publication Data

Imbriaco, Alison.
  The whooping crane : help save this endangered species! / Alison Imbriaco.
      p. cm. — (Saving endangered species)
  Includes bibliographical references.
  ISBN 1-59845-032-8
  1. Whooping crane—Juvenile literature. I. Title. II. Series.
  QL696.G84I43 2006
  598.3'2—dc22

                                        2005009005

Printed in the United States of America

10 9 8 7 6 5 4 3 2 1

To Our Readers:
Through the purchase of this book, you and your library gain access to the Report Links that specifically
back up this book.
The Publisher will provide access to the Report Links that back up this book and will keep these Report
Links up to date on **www.myreportlinks.com** for five years from the book's first publication date.
We have done our best to make sure all Internet addresses in this book were active and appropriate when
we went to press. However, the author and the Publisher have no control over, and assume no liability
for, the material available on those Internet sites or on other Web sites they may link to.
The usage of the MyReportLinks.com Books Web site is subject to the terms and conditions stated on the
Usage Policy Statement on **www.myreportlinks.com.**
A password may be required to access the Report Links that back up this book. The password is found
on the bottom of page 4 of this book.
Any comments or suggestions can be sent by e-mail to comments@myreportlinks.com or to the address
on the back cover.

Photo Credits: © Corel Corporation, pp. 55, 106, 113; Alberta Sustainable Resource Development,
p. 47; American Museum of Natural History, p. 39; CBS News.com, p. 11; Cornell Lab of Ornithology,
p. 53; Defenders of Wildlife, p. 51; Enslow Publishers, Inc., pp. 5, 6–7; Environment Canada, pp. 15,
65; Florida Fish and Wildlife Conservation Commission, p. 36; Hinterland Who's Who, p. 74; International
Crane Foundation, pp. 29, 42, 66, 92; Journey North, p. 83; MyReportLinks.com Books, p. 4; National
Audubon Society, p. 59; National Park Service, p. 43; National Wildlife Federation, p. 26; National
Wildlife Refuge Association, p. 45; Natural Resources Foundation of Wisconsin, p. 109; *Nature,* p. 91;
North American Bird Conservation Initiative, p. 111; Operation Migration, Inc., pp. 13, 40, 85, 86, 89,
101; Parks Canada, p. 25; Photos.com, pp. 21, 49, 57, 78; Platte River Whooping Crane Maintenance
Trust, Inc., p. 38; Roger Tory Peterson Institute, p. 63; Rowe Sanctuary, p. 17; Theodore Roosevelt
Association, p. 61; United States Fish and Wildlife Service, pp. 19, 33, 69, 115; United States Geological
Survey, Patuxent Wildlife Research Center, pp. 1, 3, 24, 31, 35, 72, 77, 80, 95, 97, 103; Whooping Crane
Conservation Association, p. 107; Whooping Crane Eastern Partnership, pp. 9, 99.

Cover Photos: United States Geological Survey, Patuxent Wildlife Research Center; Photos.com.

CONTENTS

MyReportLinks.com Books
Great Books, Great Links, Great for Research!

The Internet sites featured in this book can save you hours of research time. These Internet sites—we call them **"Report Links"**—are constantly changing, but we keep them up to date on our Web site.

When you see this "Approved Web Site" logo, you will know that we are directing you to a great Internet site that will help you with your research.

Give it a try! Type http://www.myreportlinks.com into your browser, click on the series title and enter the password, then click on the book title, and scroll down to the Report Links listed for this book.

The Report Links will bring you to great source documents, photographs, and illustrations. MyReportLinks.com Books save you time, feature Report Links that are kept up to date, and make report writing easier than ever! A complete listing of the Report Links can be found on pages 116–117 at the back of the book.

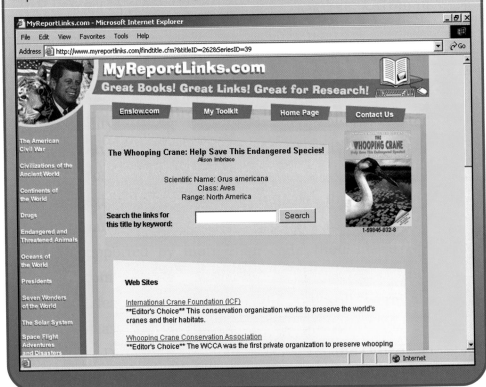

Please see "To Our Readers" on the copyright page for important information about this book, the MyReportLinks.com Web site, and the Report Links that back up this book.

Please enter SWC1027 if asked for a password.

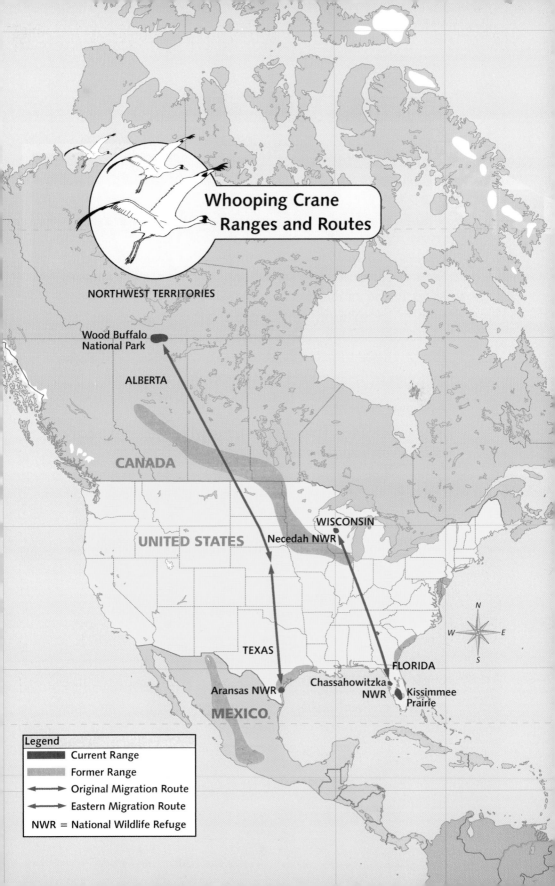

WHOOPING CRANE FACTS

▶ **Scientific Name**

Grus americana

▶ **Range**

North America. The whooping crane was first listed as endangered in 1967. The United States Fish and Wildlife Service currently lists the whooping crane as endangered in its entire range except where it is listed as an experimental population. In Canada, whooping cranes are protected under SARA (the Species at Risk Act), the Migratory Birds Convention Act, the National Parks Act, and by legislation in provinces and territories.

▶ **Average Height**

At about five feet (two meters), the whooping crane is the tallest North American bird.

▶ **Average Weight**

14 to 17 pounds (6 to 8 kilograms)

▶ **Wingspan**

About seven feet (two meters)

▶ **Physical Description**

Adults: White feathers with black wing tips that are hidden when cranes stand; red forehead or crown, which is a patch of rough skin with sparse black hairlike feathers; black cheeks. Males and females are similar in appearance.

Immature: Feathers are cinnamon and white; immature cranes lack the red crown.

▶ **Life Span**

Between 22 and 24 years in the wild; up to 70 years in captivity

▶ Habitat

Marshy wetlands

▶ Eggs

About four inches (ten centimeters) long, weighing about seven ounces (two hundred grams). Soft blue, gray-green, or tan; brown splotches for camouflage. Females usually lay two eggs in a mound of reeds and marsh grass; the eggs are incubated by both male and female for about a month.

▶ Current Population

As of January 2005—328 whooping cranes in the wild: 213 in the Wood Buffalo National Park/Aransas National Wildlife Refuge population, 46 in the Wisconsin/Florida population, and 69 in the central Florida population. There are 109 whooping cranes in captivity, including 29 nesting pairs.

▶ Migration

The original wild migratory flock flies from Wood Buffalo, Alberta, Canada, to Aransas National Wildlife Refuge, Texas—a 2,700-mile (4,344-kilometer) journey that takes about two months. In 2001, an experimental eastern migratory population was established. This population migrates from the Necedah National Wildlife Refuge in Wisconsin to the Chassahowitzka National Wildlife Refuge in Florida, a journey of about 1,250 miles (2,012 kilometers).

▶ Threats

Loss of wetlands habitat, collisions with power lines, human disturbance, poaching and accidental shooting by hunters, predators

For the whooping crane there is no freedom but that of unbounded wilderness, no life except its own. Without meekness, without a sign of humility, it has refused to accept our idea of what the world should be like.

Robert Porter Allen, *The Whooping Crane*

Chapter 1 ▶

A HISTORY-MAKING FLIGHT

In the early light of a crisp October morning, seven young whooping cranes watch from their pen as an ultralight aircraft taxis down a grassy runway and takes off. A second ultralight taxis behind the first one. (Ultralights

http://www.bringbackthecranes.org/media/info_kit/Education/circle-pen.jpg - Microsoft Internet Explorer

File   Edit   View   Favorites   Tools   Help

Address http://www.bringbackthecranes.org/media/info_kit/Education/circle-pen.jpg   Go

Done

Here, young whoopers are trained to follow an ultralight aircraft flown by a costumed pilot. A group of conservation organizations known as the **Whooping Crane Eastern Partnership** (WCEP) are working together to help the endangered whooping crane. Read more about their efforts at the WCEP site.

EDITOR'S CHOICE

are small, single-seat aircraft, carrying little fuel, whose weight and speed can vary, depending on the country they are operating in. In the United States, ultralights cannot weigh more than 254 pounds or fly faster than 63 miles per hour.)

The six-month-old whooping cranes know the *whirr* of the ultralight's engine; they first heard it before they even hatched from their eggs. Almost as soon as the birds were able to walk, they followed an ultralight on the ground. When they learned to fly, they followed the ultralight into the air. On this day, they will follow the familiar aircraft on a flight that will make history.

As the second ultralight taxis toward the cranes' pen, costumed handlers quickly open the door to the enclosure so that the young cranes can form up behind the little aircraft. As ultralight pilot Joseph Duff explained, "The timing of a take-off is critical. We have to wait long enough for all the birds to come out of the pen so we don't leave any behind, yet not too long to allow the birds to get ahead of us, or the take-off run must be aborted for fear of running into them."[1]

Soon the young cranes are flying behind the two lead ultralight planes. They will stay in the wake of the ultralights' wings where they find less air resistance. A third ultralight follows behind to pick up any stragglers or follow a crane that might decide to take a break. The flight this morning lasts about forty-five minutes and covers less than thirty miles (forty-eight kilometers), but it is a giant step toward a better future for whooping cranes.

▶ Learning to Migrate

In 2001, a handful of young whooping cranes followed ultralight aircraft from Wisconsin to Florida. The 1,228-mile (1,976-kilometer) trip took almost seven weeks. As they flew, the young cranes learned a migration route that no whooping crane has followed for many generations. Cranes are born with a migration instinct, but the instinct needs to be "triggered" by older cranes who teach the migration route to young cranes.

Whooping cranes disappeared from the eastern half of North America many years ago, and all eastern migration routes were lost to the birds. Then two Canadians proved that they could use ultralight aircraft to teach birds to migrate. The men, Bill Lishman and Joe Duff, first led Canada geese south in 1993. In 2001, they led a

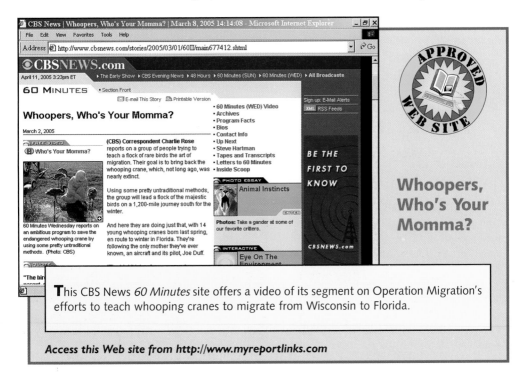

This CBS News *60 Minutes* site offers a video of its segment on Operation Migration's efforts to teach whooping cranes to migrate from Wisconsin to Florida.

Access this Web site from http://www.myreportlinks.com

small cohort, or family group, of young whooping cranes from Wisconsin to Florida using ultralight aircraft.

Five of the young whoopers survived the winter on their own in Florida. When they returned to Wisconsin by themselves the next spring, they proved that it is possible to establish an eastern population of wild whooping cranes. They became the foundation of the second migratory flock in North America—a flock that will greatly increase the chances of the species' survival.

▶ *Grus americana*

The whooping crane, whose scientific name is *Grus americana,* is one of the most elegant birds in the world. It is also one of the funniest looking. Viewed head on, the whooper's head looks small at the end of its long, olive-gray bill. On the top of its head, a red "cap" is actually a patch of rough skin with just a few black hairlike feathers. This cap changes color, from a dull plum to a vivid red, depending on the crane's mood. Another red stripe outlines the crane's bill, and black patches outline the sides of its face.

Most of the whooping crane's 5-foot (1.5-meter) height is in its long legs and long neck. The feathers on the adult whooping crane are white, except for black primary feathers at the tips of its extended wings. When the crane stands with wings folded at its sides, the black tips are invisible.

The whooping crane is especially beautiful in flight. Its wings span 7 to 8 feet (2 to 2.5 meters), and the black primary feathers separate and twist gracefully as the

▲ The majesty of a whooping crane is captured in this photograph taken by Operation Migration during the eastern flock's 2004 fall migration south. This whooper is flying over Georgia, not far from its final destination of Florida.

crane catches thermals, rising currents of warm air, and soars like an eagle. As it flies, the crane extends its neck forward and its legs behind as its mighty wings carry it through the air.

The birds are named for their loud, resonant "whooping" call that can be heard as far away as two miles.

▶ A History of Decline

Grus americana exists only in North America. The tall, white wading birds live in marshy wetlands and migrate from summer nesting grounds to winter feeding areas farther south. Before Europeans began to settle the continent, whooping cranes probably nested from Illinois north to north central Ontario, Canada, and west through the states of the central prairies and into central Alberta, Canada. Winter homes probably ranged from the highlands of central Mexico to the eastern seacoast of the United States, from New Jersey to Florida.

Naturalists estimate that about fifteen hundred whooping cranes lived in North America before the first European colonists arrived. The number soon declined as more European settlers arrived in the New World. The fiercely territorial cranes require large nesting areas far from human disturbance. Hunting and egg collection and draining of marshy areas to make farmland also led to the cranes' decline.

By 1870, according to estimates, the total whooping crane population had dropped to fewer than seven hundred birds.[2] By 1941, only about fifteen birds migrated from an unknown nesting location to a winter home on the coast of Texas. A flock of nonmigrating cranes in southwestern Louisiana had dwindled to only eleven birds in 1938. Most of the remaining whoopers of that nonmigratory flock were lost in a hurricane, and the last one was captured in 1949.[3]

▶ An Important Discovery

In 1954, a biologist discovered the cranes' summer nesting home in a nearly uninhabited part of northwestern Canada. There, in an area of Wood Buffalo National Park called the Peace-Athabasca Delta, the cranes used a marshy region of about five hundred to six hundred

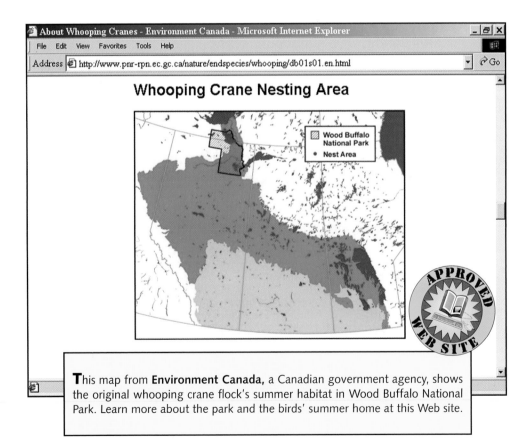

This map from **Environment Canada,** a Canadian government agency, shows the original whooping crane flock's summer habitat in Wood Buffalo National Park. Learn more about the park and the birds' summer home at this Web site.

square miles (thirteen hundred to sixteen hundred square kilometers).[4]

Thirteen years later, crane specialists began a program that they hoped would help the species survive. Because the small wild flock is so vulnerable to natural or man-made catastrophes, conservationists wanted to be sure that enough whoopers lived in other locations to preserve the species. In 1967, researchers began looking for whooper nests and removing one egg from each clutch of two. The "borrowed" eggs were then hatched and raised in captivity.

In 1993, crane specialists were able to begin programs designed to start new wild flocks. By the end of 2004, about 105 whooping cranes lived in new flocks established in the wild. The original wild flock numbered 213. In addition, just over one hundred cranes are kept in captivity, and these cranes provide eggs for new release programs.

What You Can Do to Help Whoopers Survive

Whooping cranes survive today because humans cared enough about these birds when they were nearly extinct to take action. If they are to continue to survive, they will continue to need our help.

What can you do to help save whooping cranes? First, learn more about them: where they live, what kind of habitat they need, what they eat, and how they are affected by the things we do. One way to learn about cranes is to visit the places where they live. Whooping cranes are raised in captivity and studied at the Patuxent

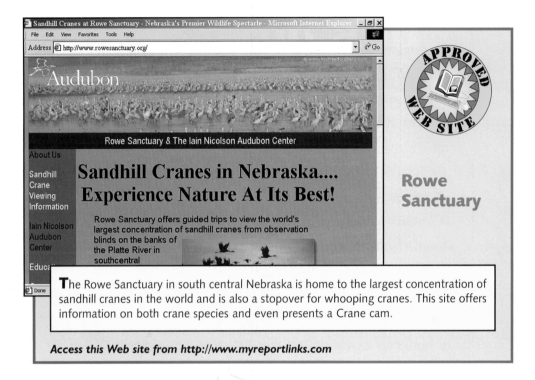

Sandhill Cranes at Rowe Sanctuary - Nebraska's Premier Wildlife Spectacle - Microsoft Internet Explorer

File   Edit   View   Favorites   Tools   Help

Address http://www.rowesanctuary.org/

Audubon

Rowe Sanctuary & The Iain Nicolson Audubon Center

About Us

Sandhill
Crane
Viewing
Information

Iain Nicolson
Audubon
Center

Educa...

Sandhill Cranes in Nebraska....
Experience Nature At Its Best!

Rowe Sanctuary offers guided trips to view the world's
largest concentration of sandhill cranes from observation
blinds on the banks of
the Platte River in
southcentral

**Rowe
Sanctuary**

The Rowe Sanctuary in south central Nebraska is home to the largest concentration of sandhill cranes in the world and is also a stopover for whooping cranes. This site offers information on both crane species and even presents a Crane cam.

Access this Web site from http://www.myreportlinks.com

Wildlife Research Center in Maryland, the International Crane Foundation in Wisconsin, and the Devonian Wildlife Conservation Center in Calgary, Canada. The San Antonio Zoo, the New Orleans Zoo, the Audubon Center for Research on Endangered Species (ACRES) in Louisiana, and the Lowry Park Zoo in Florida also have whooping cranes on public display.

Viewing cranes in the wild is not easy, though, because the birds are very private. At the Aransas National Wildlife Refuge in Texas, where the original wild flock of whooping cranes spends the winter, a tall viewing platform offers the possibility of a sighting, and boat tours take people close to the cranes.

Another place to see whooping cranes during their spring and fall migrations is in the National Audubon

Society's Rowe Sanctuary, situated on the Platte River in Nebraska. Whooping cranes stop there along their migration route. Observation blinds, which look a little like tree houses, have been constructed to allow people to watch the cranes without disturbing them.

People fortunate enough to live close to the Rowe Sanctuary might choose to become part of the Whooper Watch, a program started in 2001 by the National Wildlife Federation and the Nebraska Wildlife Federation. During the months of spring and fall migration, the trained volunteers of Whooper Watch get up early in the morning, three or four times a week, and drive one of twenty-six routes in search of whooping cranes. The information they gather helps environmentalists develop plans to maintain the Platte River migration stop.

Since the spring of 2002, an observation tower at Wisconsin's Necedah National Wildlife Refuge offers visitors views of the new eastern migratory population of whooping cranes on their return north. In the early morning, they can be seen foraging along the shores of East Rynearson Pond.

▶ Spotting a Whooper in the Wild

Because whooping cranes are now flying along new migration routes, the chances of seeing one in the wild are increasing. It is important that you know what you are seeing and what you should—and should not—do.

If you see a whooper in the wild, stay away from it. Crane specialists who have been working to reintroduce

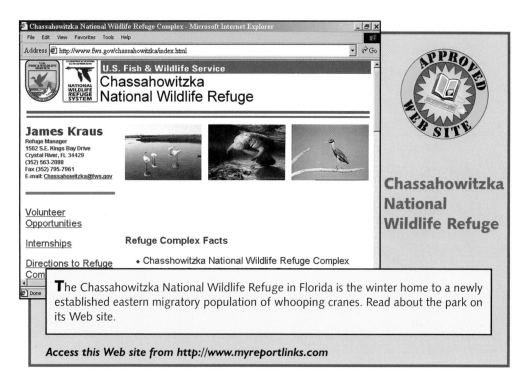

Chassahowitzka
National
Wildlife Refuge

The Chassahowitzka National Wildlife Refuge in Florida is the winter home to a newly established eastern migratory population of whooping cranes. Read about the park on its Web site.

Access this Web site from http://www.myreportlinks.com

whooping cranes into the wild have taken precautions to prevent the cranes from becoming friendly with humans. If they are to survive in the wild, cranes need to learn to do so on their own.

The Whooping Crane Eastern Partnership, a group of organizations that is working to reintroduce whooping cranes into the wild, asks people to stay at least 600 feet (183 meters) away from a crane they might encounter. They recommend that people remain concealed and speak softly so that the cranes will not be disturbed. Finally, they ask people not to trespass on private property in their attempts to see whooping cranes.[5] Many landowners generously share their land with migrating whooping cranes, but they might reconsider if having whooping cranes means having trespassers as well.

At the same time, crane specialists want very much to know where the cranes are. Many of the reintroduced cranes have been fitted with radio transmitters, but the batteries often run out and do not always work. If you see a whooping crane, you can help by contacting your county's or state's Department of Natural Resources office to report your sighting.

Wildlife Refuges

Whooping cranes would probably be extinct today if it were not for national wildlife refuges that offer them habitat and protection. Learning about the refuges, what they do, and what is required to maintain them is an essential first step in making decisions about them. Unfortunately, the National Wildlife Refuge System in the United States is often not considered a priority when the federal government decides how to spend money.

What can you do? Learn who your representatives in government are and how they vote on environmental issues. You can let them know that you think wildlife refuges are important, so that these legislators will remember to consider the refuges when they vote on issues that affect the environment.

Water Conservation

There are even more important things you can do closer to home to help whooping cranes. Look for ways that you and your family and your community can conserve water. Whooping cranes live in wetlands, and they depend on wetland habitat for survival. As our human population keeps growing, we make increasing demands

▲ *Fighting water pollution is one very important way in which you can help whooping cranes survive.*

on our environment, including wetlands. Finding ways to conserve water and to keep rivers and streams free of pollution may be the most important thing you or anyone can do to help whooping cranes and other wetlands animals survive.

▶ Fighting Pollution Close to Home

You can begin by making sure that your own yard is not adding to the pollution that happens each time it rains. When rains cannot soak completely into the ground, storm-water runoff is produced. A certain amount of runoff is expected, but reducing it is easy and important. When storm water runs off of surfaces such as roads and driveways and even manicured lawns, it carries pollutants such as sediment, fertilizers, oil, gasoline, and animal waste that enter streams and rivers. You can reduce the amount of runoff by simply cleaning up after your pet and by never dumping anything down a storm drain. You can also encourage your parents to use fertilizers and pesticides sparingly, if at all, and to use plants native to your region, since these require less water and fertilizing.

If your community sponsors events that involve cleaning up local rivers, streams, or ponds and the areas that border them, consider becoming involved. You may not have had any part in polluting a body of water, but you can definitely take part in helping to clean one up. The actions you take today, even for just a few hours, may make the difference in a whooper's chance for survival in the long term.

Chapter 2

WHOOPING CRANES IN THE WILD

Far in the north of Canada, deep in the marshes of Wood Buffalo National Park, a mother whooping crane lays one large egg. It is early May, but the temperature still drops below freezing at night. To keep the egg warm, the mother whooping crane and her mate take turns sitting on the nest, or brooding, to protect the egg with their body heat. Within a few days, the mother crane lays a second egg.

Each egg is about four inches (ten centimeters) long and weighs about seven ounces (two hundred grams). Tan splotches on the gray-green eggs help them blend into the colors of the nest. In other whooping crane nests, the eggs may be a soft blue with tan or brown splotches.

▶ The Nest

Home for these eggs is a large nest made from woven reeds and marsh grass. The nest, which sits in shallow water, looks like a foot-high mound of dead reeds. But few eyes will see it in the rushes and cattails of the marshy area. Both whooper parents worked to build the nest, gathering the reeds and grass with their long bills

▲ *A whooping crane's nest can measure up to five feet across.*

and pushing the bits of vegetation into place. When the mound is high enough and 2 to 5 feet (1 to 2 meters) across, the cranes make a shallow cavity for the eggs. If the whoopers have been parents before, they may rebuild last year's nest. The cranes return to the same territory to breed year after year.

Around the nest, the marshes stretch for miles, providing an ideal isolated home for the last wild flock of whooping cranes. The Peace-Athabasca Delta, one of the largest inland freshwater deltas in the world, is formed by three large rivers: the Peace, Athabasca, and Slave rivers.[1] In the freshwater streams, marshes, mudflats, and shallow oxbow lakes of this delta, the cranes find food and protection.

For a month, the whooping crane parents take turns on the nest, sitting still for two hours or so and standing occasionally to use their long beaks to turn the eggs over. As they brood, they sometimes make a low purring sound, known as a brooding call. From inside the egg, the chick hears her parents.

Protecting the Nest

The male whooping crane has the primary responsibility for protecting the nest. He has claimed a territory of

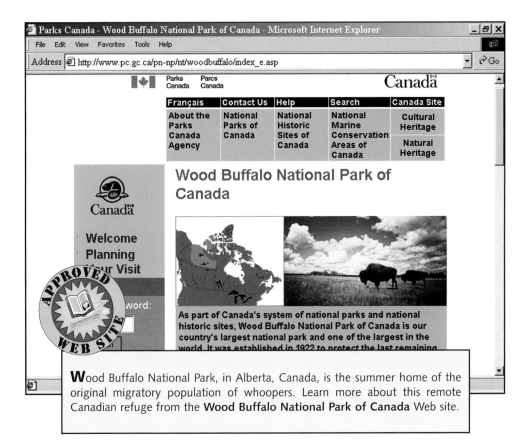

Wood Buffalo National Park, in Alberta, Canada, is the summer home of the original migratory population of whoopers. Learn more about this remote Canadian refuge from the **Wood Buffalo National Park of Canada** Web site.

almost three square miles (eight square kilometers), and he patrols it diligently.[2] He watches for foxes, wolverines, wolves, and bears on the ground. Other predators, such as owls and eagles, come from the sky. He also drives away other cranes that would compete for the food his family will need.

Whoopers are fiercely protective of their territories. When a male whooping crane sees an intruder approaching, he begins a "low-density" aggressive display to inform the intruder that he is ready to fight. His red skin cap expands and becomes redder as he stands tall, with his head held high and the red cap turned to the

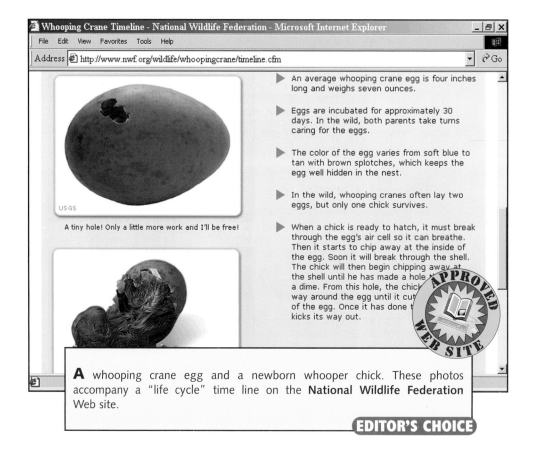

Whooping Crane Timeline - National Wildlife Federation - Microsoft Internet Explorer

File   Edit   View   Favorites   Tools   Help

Address http://www.nwf.org/wildlife/whoopingcrane/timeline.cfm   Go

USGS

A tiny hole! Only a little more work and I'll be free!

▶ An average whooping crane egg is four inches long and weighs seven ounces.

▶ Eggs are incubated for approximately 30 days. In the wild, both parents take turns caring for the eggs.

▶ The color of the egg varies from soft blue to tan with brown splotches, which keeps the egg well hidden in the nest.

▶ In the wild, whooping cranes often lay two eggs, but only one chick survives.

▶ When a chick is ready to hatch, it must break through the egg's air cell so it can breathe. Then it starts to chip away at the inside of the egg. Soon it will break through the shell. The chick will then begin chipping away at the shell until he has made a hole the size of a dime. From this hole, the chick works its way around the egg until it cuts the top off of the egg. Once it has done this, the chick kicks its way out.

A whooping crane egg and a newborn whooper chick. These photos accompany a "life cycle" time line on the **National Wildlife Federation** Web site.

EDITOR'S CHOICE

intruder. The crane accompanies the visual display with a purring rattle, which is unmistakably menacing. If the intruder does not leave immediately, the whooper begins a ritualized display walk of steps that are both exaggerated and rhythmic.[3] Naturalists refer to this display as strutting. As he struts, the whooper bobs his bill up and down in time with his steps, fans his toes, and raises his tail feathers to form a bustle.

The aggressive display often includes a lift and ruffling of the crane's feathers until his whole body shakes. He also sounds a sharp, loud guard call.[4] The display itself is often enough to send an intruder away, especially if it has encountered a whooping crane before.

If the intruder has not taken the hint, the crane will suddenly rush at it, flapping his wings as he glides over the ground. The rush might end with more ruffling of the feathers—or it might end with an attack. Whooping cranes attack by spearing an enemy with their sharp bills, jumping into the air to slash the enemy with their inner toenails in a maneuver known as a jump rake, or thrashing the enemy with their massive wings. If the intruder is another crane, it will avoid a fight by cowering in a submissive posture as it leaves.

The Egg Hatches

Finally, about thirty days after laying the first egg, the mother whooping crane hears sounds coming from inside the egg. Curled up inside, the chick answers her mother's brood call as she begins the long ordeal that will get her out of the egg. First, she breaks through to an air cell in the large end of the egg and begins to breathe. Then the chick must break through the shell to get more air. The chick pecks at the shell until she makes a star-shaped crack called a star pip.

Pecking through the eggshell to make the star pip is hard work, and the chick is exhausted. For the next twenty-four hours, she rests inside the egg. Then she goes back to work on the star pip, pecking at the crack until the hole is about the size of a dime. Finally, the chick is ready to break the egg. She pecks in a line around the large end of the egg, turning completely around as she goes. Making a break line around the egg might seem like the hardest task of all, but it only takes about an hour. Then the chick kicks her way out of the egg. As she turns and kicks inside the egg, her body absorbs the yolk sac, which will provide nourishment until she learns to eat.

The hatched chick is a pitiful sight. The cinnamon-colored downy hair that covers her body is wet, and her legs are swollen. The chick weighs only 4 to 5 ounces (113 to 142 grams) and could fit in a person's hand. Her eyes are blue, but they are closed.

▶ First Lessons

While the chick was in the egg, her parents spent long hours sitting very still on the nest. Once the chick has hatched, however, the adult whooping cranes have little time to sit still. First, they need to teach their offspring how to drink, which they do by dipping their beaks into water and letting the water drip from them. Chicks are

Learn more about whooping crane chicks at the Web site of the **International Crane Foundation.**

EDITOR'S CHOICE

attracted to the shape of their parents' bills. They are also attracted to the moving water. As the chick tries to catch the water drops, she will get her first drink by accident. This lesson may take hours as the parents patiently dip and drip.[5] The lesson is tedious but necessary. Chicks easily become dehydrated, and when they do, they lose interest in eating.

The Second Egg

By the time the first chick has kicked her way out of the egg, the second chick begins pecking the egg to make the star pip—except that the second chick may not survive for long. Whooping cranes usually lay two eggs, but the chicks require so much food and care that the parents often raise only one chick—if they are lucky. A healthy first chick is bigger than a younger sibling, able to snatch all the food the parents bring. The smaller chick may starve, be accidentally trampled, or be pushed out of the nest.

Parenting Whooper Style

One chick is enough to keep both parents busy. They need to catch food for the chick all day, and they need to protect her while she is still small enough to be a tender mouthful for a wolverine or an eagle. The whoopers bring their offspring such appetizing tidbits as insects, small fish, worms, toads, and mice, as well as some plants and berries. Whooping cranes are omnivores—they eat just about anything they find. The parents teach the chick to eat the same way they teach her to drink, by patiently picking up pieces of food in their long bills so the chick will peck at it and learn what it is.

The chick is able to swim within a day or so of hatching. That way, she will be able to keep up with her parents. Her legs will have to grow quite a bit for her to walk as fast as adult cranes, who cover a yard with each step.

Communicating

The chick is also noisy, peeping loudly when it is hungry. The chick's shrill peeping sounds nothing like the trumpeting call of its parents. As a crane grows to adulthood,

This five-day-old chick raised at the Patuxent Wildlife Research Center in Laurel, Maryland, has already learned to eat from a bowl, thanks to his "parents," a stuffed model and a puppet head.

its trachea, or windpipe, grows very long—in fact, it grows to about five feet (two meters), which is as long as the whooping crane is tall. The trachea coils inside the whooper's chest cavity, protected by the breastbone. It is this extra-long windpipe that gives the whooping crane its loud and resonant call.

In addition to the high-pitched "feed me!" call, the newly hatched chick also has a stress call, which tells the parents she is frightened, cold, or lost. Another call is a contact call that imitates the parents' communication. Although they are very capable of drowning out the chick with their loud whooping call, the whooper parents "talk" to their chick with low purring sounds. One crane expert noted that naturalists have described about twenty-seven different calls between a whooper chick and its parents.[6]

Foraging

During the first days of her life, the chick will stay close to the nest. When the chick gets cold, her mother will invite her to come under her wing to warm her with her body heat. As soon as the chick can keep up, when she is about ten days old, the parents lead her away from the nest. She will accompany her parents as they forage all day for food for themselves and for her.

As the crane parents forage, they communicate with each other frequently, using low purring noises. If they become separated, one will call and immediately be answered by the mate. The chick may affirm her connection to her parents by pecking at their long bills.

▶ Growing

The chick needs to eat a lot so that she can grow quickly. She needs to be ready in only four or five months to make the long migratory flight to the winter home in Texas, about twenty-seven hundred miles (forty-three hundred kilometers) away. By the time the chick is a month old, she will be about two feet (one meter) tall and will weigh almost 5 pounds (2.3 kilograms). Two weeks later, when she is about forty-five days old, she will have grown another foot and gained about three pounds (one kilogram). Her blue eyes are beginning to turn aquamarine. When she is six months old, her eyes will be golden.

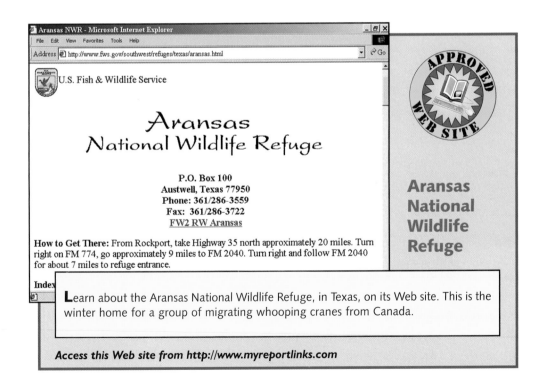

Learn about the Aransas National Wildlife Refuge, in Texas, on its Web site. This is the winter home for a group of migrating whooping cranes from Canada.

Access this Web site from http://www.myreportlinks.com

Brown and white feathers begin to emerge through the chick's down, or soft feathers, when the whooping crane chick is about a month and a half old. The young whooper now needs to learn a new skill called preening. This process often begins with a bath. Cranes use their bills to nibble at the base of a feather and then draw the feather through the bill to keep it smooth and clean.[7] A gland at the base of a crane's tail contains oil, and the crane uses its bill and head to rub this oil into its back and wing feathers.[8] As the young chick preens her new feathers, she will wash away the baby down from them.

▷ Unison Calling

As the chick follows her parents through the marshes, she sometimes sees them engage in a duet that naturalists refer to as unison calling. The unison call is actually a long series of different whooping calls sounded by both cranes as they stand tall and close together, with their bills pointed toward the sky. Each crane has a separate part in the call. The female usually begins and then makes two or three calls for each one of the male's calls.[9] A whooping crane pair might sound its unison call when threatened by an intruder or as a way of affirming its bond. Each pair has a distinct unison call that can be distinguished from the calls of other pairs.[10] (Naturalists record unison calls to provide a way of identifying whooping cranes. This process is called voice printing.)

The unison call may be accompanied by a dance, although all cranes dance, whether or not they have a

▲ *The dance of a pair of whooping cranes is amazing to behold.*

mate. The dance may include bowing, jumping, running, stick or grass tossing, and wing flapping.

Whooping crane pairs perform their unison calls throughout the year, but they tend to be quieter while they are raising a chick and when they molt.

▶ Fledging

Although the chick is growing feathers and long wings, she cannot yet fly. At this time, neither can her parents. In late summer, whoopers molt, shedding their feathers so that new ones can grow in.

During her first months, the young whooper is very vulnerable to predators. She cannot fly away, and she is not big enough to protect herself, so she is completely dependent upon her parents for protection. As careful as whooping crane parents try to be, many chicks do not survive these early weeks. Although the chick is learning to find food for herself as she follows her parents through the marshes, her parents give her most of the food she eats.

At about ten weeks, the young whooper takes her first short flight. She has fledged, or learned to fly. Flying requires practice, and the fledgling crane will practice often in the coming weeks. She has only a month to

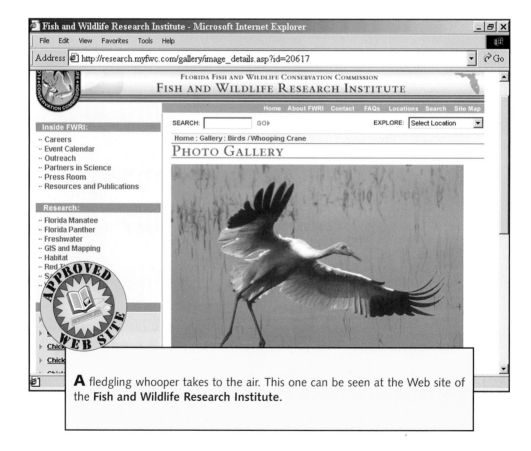

A fledgling whooper takes to the air. This one can be seen at the Web site of the **Fish and Wildlife Research Institute.**

become a strong enough flier to accompany her parents on the long migration to Texas.

To get airborne, cranes take a couple of running steps to build momentum before they spring into the air. As they flap their long wings, they set a distinctive rhythm with a quick upstroke and a slower downstroke. Whooping cranes can fly as fast as 45 miles per hour (72 kilometers per hour). The long black primary feathers at the ends of their wings twist and separate in the air currents, accenting the strength of the great wings.

Fledging brings another call to the young crane's vocabulary. As the crane stands erect, facing into the wind, and prepares to fly, its call is brief but steady.[11]

The Migration

September's cooler nights tell the whooping cranes that it is almost time for them to head south. When the day of departure has come, the mother, father, and young crane will take off together. The family may join another small whooper group, or it may not. Although the whoopers' migration route is fairly narrow and all the cranes will follow the same route, they migrate in small family groups rather than in a large flock.

For a family with a fledgling, the migration will take about two months. Adult whoopers can easily cover more than 200 miles (322 kilometers) a day, but fledglings are not as strong and need to stop sooner.

For the cranes, an important consideration along the way is where to spend the night. Uninhabited wetlands along the route are becoming more scarce. A recently

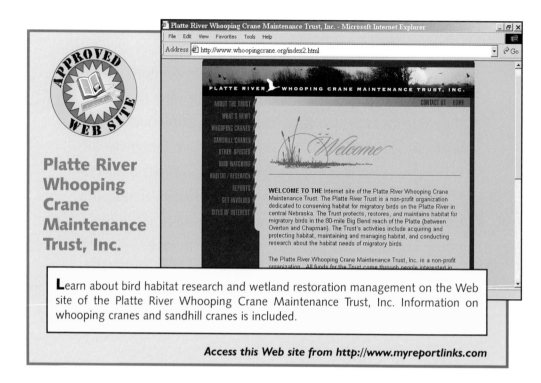

Platte River Whooping Crane Maintenance Trust, Inc.

WELCOME TO THE Internet site of the Platte River Whooping Crane Maintenance Trust. The Platte River Trust is a non-profit organization dedicated to conserving habitat for migratory birds on the Platte River in central Nebraska. The Trust protects, restores, and maintains habitat for migratory birds in the 80-mile Big Bend reach of the Platte (between Overton and Chapman). The Trust's activities include acquiring and protecting habitat, maintaining and managing habitat, and conducting research about the habitat needs of migratory birds.

The Platte River Whooping Crane Maintenance Trust, Inc. is a non-profit organization. All funds for the Trust come through people interested in

Learn about bird habitat research and wetland restoration management on the Web site of the Platte River Whooping Crane Maintenance Trust, Inc. Information on whooping cranes and sandhill cranes is included.

Access this Web site from http://www.myreportlinks.com

harvested cornfield or a cow pasture may make a good stopover. If the cranes cannot roost in water, at least they can stand on flat open land that allows them a good view all around. Cranes will sometimes spend several days at a stopover, resting and perhaps waiting for better flying weather.

An important stopover for the cranes is the Platte River in Nebraska. There the whoopers will join thousands of sandhill cranes, the other North American crane species, as well as many other migrating birds, to feed and roost on the sandbars at night. In the past, the birds shared a 300-mile (483-kilometer) stretch of the Platte River. But the river is not what it used to be. Seventy percent of its water has been diverted for agriculture. Now the thousands of migrating birds come together each spring and autumn on an eighty-mile stretch of the river.

By the end of November or early in December, the whooper family finally arrives at its winter home in and around the Aransas National Wildlife Refuge on the Texas Gulf Coast. The 70,504-acre (28,533-hectare) refuge includes the Blackjack Peninsula, named for scattered blackjack oak trees. Here, tidal marshes broken by long narrow ponds provide good foraging areas for the cranes. The crane family will return to a specific location where the territorial birds have made "reservations" in previous years. Cranes also make winter homes on nearby

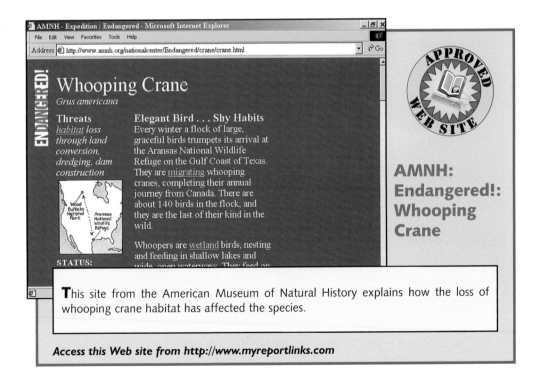

This site from the American Museum of Natural History explains how the loss of whooping crane habitat has affected the species.

Access this Web site from http://www.myreportlinks.com

Matagorda Island (which is managed by the Aransas refuge staff) and other islands and bays in the area.

Through the winter, the whooping cranes spend their time foraging for food and defending their territory. The cranes prefer to eat blue crabs, mud shrimp, and clams, but they are generally willing to eat whatever they come upon, from frogs and snakes to various plants. The fledgling's parents still feed her, although she is capable of finding food for herself. Toward the end of winter, the

▲ *In the homestretch: These whoopers, led by the pilots of Operation Migration, are flying over Georgia on the way to their new winter home in Florida.*

fledgling becomes more independent, spending more time at a distance from her parents.

The Fledgling Becomes Independent

By April, when the cranes migrate back to Wood Buffalo National Park, the young whooper is on her own. She will probably find a friend or two in her own age group to travel with. By the time she is a year old, the young whooper looks like an adult. The cinnamon-colored feathers have been replaced by white feathers, and the feathers on her head are gone, exposing the red cap.

After a year or so on her own, when she is two or three years old, she will probably find a mate. Another whooper will show interest by ruffling his feathers and strutting. He might also bob his head and make growling noises. If she is interested, she will mimic what he does, as if the two cranes are dancing together. This synchronized act is the first sign of mating.[12] The young cranes will forage close together and rest at the same time. Before settling down with a permanent mate, though, the young whooper may "date." She and her "boyfriend" may dance together, spend time side by side, and call to each other—and then break up.[13] As the young crane matures, though, she will form a permanent bond with another crane. That bond will probably last until one of the two cranes dies. If her mate dies before she does, she may take another mate.

At three years of age, the young whooper is almost an adult and probably has a mate. She and her mate may practice building nests and may build several nests in the

Free Photos - ICF - Microsoft Internet Explorer

File   Edit   View   Favorites   Tools   Help

Address http://www.savingcranes.org/photo/free/photo.cfm?p=28   Go

APPROVED WEB SITE

Done

The **International Crane Foundation** is dedicated to the preservation of crane species worldwide. Information on wetland ecology, habitat restoration, and the importance of education is also included.

EDITOR'S CHOICE

territory they defend. However, she will not lay eggs until she is four or five years old. Then, if she and her mate can protect the nest, she will become the mother on the nest, calling softly to the chick curled in his egg.

If the crane manages to avoid power lines and disease along the migration route, and if she is not killed by a predator as she defends her chick, she may live to be more than twenty years old.

Chapter 3

THREATS TO SURVIVAL

Grus americana began to disappear from the North American landscape almost as soon as the first European colonists arrived. The continent never supported a large number of whoopers to begin with, and hunting and egg collection by an increasing human population had a devastating effect on the whooping crane population.

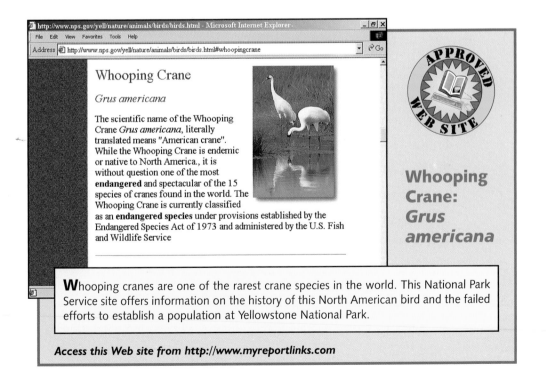

http://www.nps.gov/yell/nature/animals/birds/birds.html - Microsoft Internet Explorer

File   Edit   View   Favorites   Tools   Help

Address   http://www.nps.gov/yell/nature/animals/birds/birds.html#whoopingcrane   Go

Whooping Crane

Grus americana

The scientific name of the Whooping Crane *Grus americana*, literally translated means "American crane". While the Whooping Crane is endemic or native to North America., it is without question one of the most **endangered** and spectacular of the 15 species of cranes found in the world. The Whooping Crane is currently classified as an **endangered species** under provisions established by the Endangered Species Act of 1973 and administered by the U.S. Fish and Wildlife Service

Whooping Crane: *Grus americana*

Whooping cranes are one of the rarest crane species in the world. This National Park Service site offers information on the history of this North American bird and the failed efforts to establish a population at Yellowstone National Park.

Access this Web site from http://www.myreportlinks.com

▶ Hunting and Egg Collection

The early settlers needed food for their families. Hunters looking for dinner could hardly resist the 14- to 17-pound (6- to 8-kilogram) birds, and the fierce and noisy white cranes made easy targets. They often announced their presence with resounding *whoops* that carried for miles. Then the whoopers were as likely to defend their territory as to run away. People also collected the 4-inch (10-centimeter) eggs when they found the nests.

Hunting and egg collection were devastating for the cranes because they reproduce so slowly. Whoopers do not begin laying eggs until they are four or five years old. Then they usually lay only two eggs a year, and these eggs may not last through the month-long incubation. Animals as well as people find the eggs appetizing. If an egg does hatch, the flightless chick is easy prey for a variety of predators, such as eagles, wolves, and bobcats. As fierce as the parents are, they are not always successful in protecting their offspring.

Although it is now illegal to kill a whooping crane, cranes are still occasionally shot. Between 1989 and 2003, seven whooping cranes were killed by guns, and only three of the shootings were connected with hunting seasons. Seven may not seem like a large number, but in a species that is fighting to survive, the loss of even one crane matters.

▶ Habitat Destruction

Hunting is no longer as serious a threat to the whooping crane as it was in the past, but civilization has brought another more serious threat that is not easily resolved. Today, loss of habitat limits the number of whooping cranes that can survive in the wild. And wetlands, where whoopers make their home, continue to disappear at an alarming rate.

The North American landscape of long ago that supported thousands of whooping cranes was very different from the landscape today. For about 2 million years, until fourteen thousand years ago, glaciers advanced and retreated across North America. As glaciers melted, they left enormous amounts of water, but they also carved out areas of land and formed large lakes which, in turn, accumulated silt and became marshes and swamp forests. The shifting landscape buried huge blocks of ice. As the ice blocks slowly melted, the water formed deep

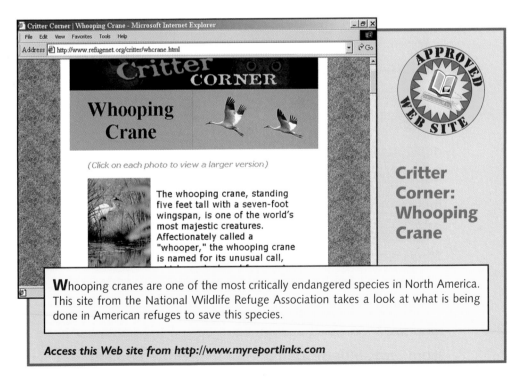

Critter Corner | Whooping Crane - Microsoft Internet Explorer

File   Edit   View   Favorites   Tools   Help

Address http://www.refugenet.org/critter/whcrane.html   Go

Critter CORNER

Whooping Crane

(Click on each photo to view a larger version)

The whooping crane, standing five feet tall with a seven-foot wingspan, is one of the world's most majestic creatures. Affectionately called a "whooper," the whooping crane is named for its unusual call,

APPROVED WEB SITE

Critter Corner: Whooping Crane

Whooping cranes are one of the most critically endangered species in North America. This site from the National Wildlife Refuge Association takes a look at what is being done in American refuges to save this species.

Access this Web site from http://www.myreportlinks.com

bogs.[1] Wetlands such as swamps and spruce bogs can be in forests. They are also found in grasslands, where they are called marshes or sedge meadows. And wetlands border every body of water.

The early colonists arriving along the East Coast found large areas of salt marshes. These flat lands prone to flooding by salt water are rich in natural resources. They provided the colonists with an abundant food supply, including fish, shellfish, and waterfowl, and marsh grasses to feed their livestock.[2] However, the abundance of food did not stop colonists from draining the marshes to grow rice and indigo plants.

As settlers moved west, they drained marshes and swamps to make land where they could farm. They found the richest wetlands in the Midwest, and those marshy meadows quickly disappeared, as did some of the now rare or extinct species, including the whooping crane and trumpeter swan, that lived in them.[3] Wetlands are now almost completely gone from the Midwestern states of Illinois and Iowa.

▶ Whoopers and Wetlands

Whoopers need large areas of wetlands. They need marshy land to raise their chicks, and they need wetlands for winter homes. During their migration, they need wetlands where they can rest and find food. As the wetlands disappeared, so did the whooping cranes.

The summer home of the original whooping crane population is in an almost uninhabited region of northern Canada. There, in Wood Buffalo National Park, they

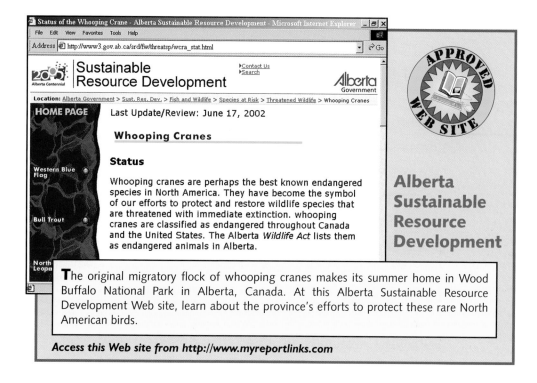

Status of the Whooping Crane - Alberta Sustainable Resource Development - Microsoft Internet Explorer

File   Edit   View   Favorites   Tools   Help

Address ⬡ http://www3.gov.ab.ca/srd/fw/threatsp/wcra_stat.html   ▼ ⟳ Go

Sustainable Resource Development

▶Contact Us
▶Search

Alberta
Government

Location: Alberta Government > Sust. Res. Dev. > Fish and Wildlife > Species at Risk > Threatened Wildlife > Whooping Cranes

HOME PAGE

Last Update/Review: June 17, 2002

Whooping Cranes

Status

Whooping cranes are perhaps the best known endangered species in North America. They have become the symbol of our efforts to protect and restore wildlife species that are threatened with immediate extinction. whooping cranes are classified as endangered throughout Canada and the United States. The Alberta *Wildlife Act* lists them as endangered animals in Alberta.

Western Blue Flag

Bull Trout

North Leopa

Alberta Sustainable Resource Development

The original migratory flock of whooping cranes makes its summer home in Wood Buffalo National Park in Alberta, Canada. At this Alberta Sustainable Resource Development Web site, learn about the province's efforts to protect these rare North American birds.

Access this Web site from http://www.myreportlinks.com

are far from humans. In fact, for years no one knew where they nested. Although this remote park straddling the border of the Northwest Territories and the province of Alberta offers large marshlands and shallow oxbow lakes, it has disadvantages, too. Because it is so far north, the breeding season is short, and it is a long way from the cranes' winter home in Texas. Whooping cranes fly up to 2,700 miles (4,344 kilometers) each spring to find the privacy and untouched wetlands they need to raise a family.

▶ Wetland Degradation

The first efforts to protect wetlands in the United States came with laws to protect the birds and waterfowl that live in them. In 1903, the first national wildlife refuge in America was established in Florida. In 1929, Congress passed the Migratory Bird Conservation Act, which provided for the purchase of private land for bird refuges.

Through the twentieth century, though, the protection of wetlands by the federal government seemed to take two steps backward for every step forward. Early in the century, with the Newlands Reclamation Act of 1902 and the Rivers and Harbors Act of 1938, the Army Corps of Engineers and the Bureau of Reclamation began to drain, fill, and dredge wetlands. In the view of naturalist and author David Rains Wallace, "These agencies have devoted as much effort (and a lot more money) to destroying wetlands as the [United States] Fish and Wildlife Service has to protecting them."[4]

Poisonous Pesticides

Wetlands suffered another setback when farmers and others began using powerful new pesticides such as DDT. DDT was developed during World War II to cut down on some of the mosquito-borne diseases that were killing soldiers. This chemical compound was very effective at killing mosquitoes and other insects. But when used on farms and residential areas, it found its way into ditches and streams that drained into wetlands, and there it stayed. Marshy areas were often sprayed directly to control mosquitoes. Through the years, DDT accumulated in the environment.

The powerful insecticide was considered safe for humans and most mammals when it was first used.

North America's wetlands, which provide habitat for whooping cranes and many other species, continue to be threatened by development and overpopulation.

But scientists soon learned that the chemical became more concentrated in the fatty tissues of animals the higher up in a food chain the animal was. So in an area of Long Island, although tiny aquatic animals such as zooplankton were found to have DDT concentrations of three parts per trillion in their tissues, ospreys and eagles were found to have DDT levels as high as 25 parts per million in their tissues.[5] Once those animals began dying, people began to question how safe DDT was. The federal government finally banned its use in 1972, after years of debate. But the damage had already been done: The coastal marshes of Long Island were found to contain thirteen pounds of DDT per acre twenty years after spraying with that insecticide.[6]

▶ Wetlands Protection

In the second half of the twentieth century, people began to realize that what they were doing to wetlands was affecting their drinking water. Scientific research revealed how much civilization depends on healthy wetlands. For example, scientists learned that swamps store water with much less evaporation than reservoirs do. They also found that marshes and swamps purify sewage discharges more cheaply than treatment plants can. And they came to realize that floodplain forests regulate stream flow more cheaply than flood-control reservoirs are able to. In other words, wetlands act as a great natural sponge, taking in and then filtering out materials that would otherwise harm the environment.

Legislation known as the Clean Water Act of 1972 required the Environmental Protection Agency (EPA) to protect wetlands as part of its responsibility to prevent water pollution. This government agency was established in 1970 after the American public became more concerned with the quality of our air, land, and water, and the effect that pollution was having on our health. But even as people began to realize the importance of wetlands, farmers were draining hundreds of thousands of wetland acres a year. In 1985, Congress passed the Food Security Act. This act withheld federal aid in the form of price-support payments and crop insurance to farmers who converted wetlands into cropland. The 1986 Tax Reform Act went further by withdrawing some tax benefits from farmers who converted wetlands.

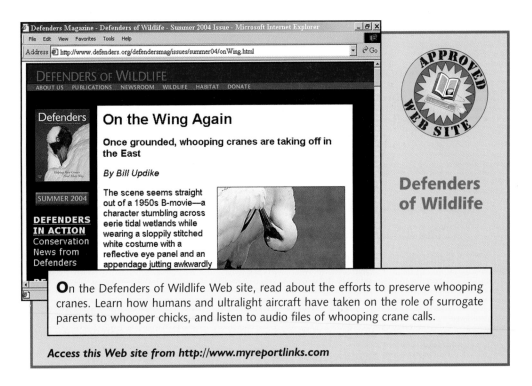

On the Defenders of Wildlife Web site, read about the efforts to preserve whooping cranes. Learn how humans and ultralight aircraft have taken on the role of surrogate parents to whooper chicks, and listen to audio files of whooping crane calls.

Access this Web site from http://www.myreportlinks.com

▶ The Demand for Water at Aransas

Fortunately for the whooping crane, efforts to preserve and even restore wetlands are ongoing. Unfortunately, competing demands for water continue to threaten the whooping cranes' habitat.

Conservationists are concerned about the health of the marshy habitat of the Aransas refuge in Texas, where the whoopers spend the winter months. To provide a healthy environment for the blue crabs, fish, clams, shrimp, and other aquatic life that whoopers (and people) eat, freshwater from rivers and streams needs to flow into the marshes and mix with the salt water from the Gulf of Mexico. However, as the human population grows, so does its demand for water. So much water is now taken from the rivers and streams in the area before they reach the marshy coastline that the balance of freshwater and salt water is threatened.

Conservationists turned to the Texas Legislature for a legal solution. Eventually the legislature was persuaded to study the conservationists' request. However, applications to take additional water from the rivers continued to be approved.[7]

▶ Problems at the Platte

The Platte River in Nebraska offers another dramatic example of conflicting demands for water. When the first settlers saw the Platte River, they described a river that was "a mile wide and a foot deep."[8] In those days, melting snow surging eastward from the Rocky Mountains every spring cleaned the river of silt and vegetation.

Many sandbars in the wide, open river provided ideal resting places for migrating whooping cranes and sandhill cranes.

By the mid-1860s, early settlers were digging ditches to take water from the Platte. The land along the Platte was rich farmland; all it needed was water. In 1909, a large dam was constructed in Wyoming, blocking the North Platte. By 1970, after the last dam had been built and a large irrigation system was set up, about 70 percent of the water that had once reached the area used by migrating birds was being diverted. Now that the river is divided into narrow channels that lie between sandbar islands filled with overgrown trees, melting snows can no longer refresh and replenish the Platte. Roosting sites at the river bottom are also much harder to come by.[9]

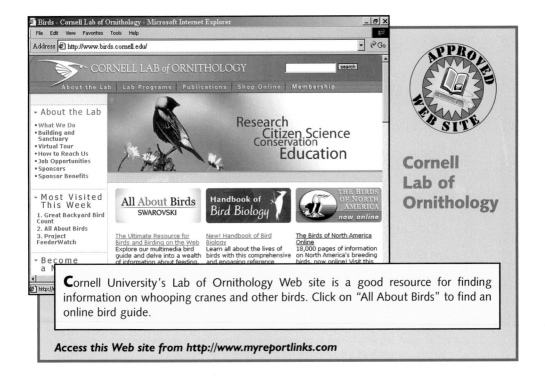

Cornell University's Lab of Ornithology Web site is a good resource for finding information on whooping cranes and other birds. Click on "All About Birds" to find an online bird guide.

Access this Web site from http://www.myreportlinks.com

Problems in the Peace-Athabasca Delta

Even in remote northern Canada, the marshes that provide a summer home for whoopers are changing. The delta's ecosystem requires yearly flooding, but during the past twenty-five years, several prolonged periods of drought have dried up some of the marshy areas. The first dry period followed the construction and filling of a hydroelectric dam at the headwaters of the Peace River. Then a few years later, scientists noticed that the spring flood of 1974 was less than the marshes needed.

Experts have since learned that carefully timing the release of water from the dam can increase the floods caused by melting ice blocks. Fortunately for the whoopers, Canadian scientists continue to study the condition of the huge inland delta to protect and preserve it.[10]

The Overall Effect of Pollution

Can you imagine a river so filled with toxins that it was actually on fire? That is exactly what happened in Cleveland, Ohio, not so long ago. The United States has made great progress in cleaning up its rivers since the day in 1969 that the Cuyahoga River in Cleveland caught fire because it was so full of industrial pollutants. However, keeping pollution out of rivers is proving to be difficult. Laws may regulate industrial pollution, but much of the pollution finding its way into bodies of water comes from roads, parking lots, and farms. Toxic pollutants may rise into the air in the form of dust and then descend in raindrops. Water pollution affects the whooping cranes directly because it kills the food they eat, especially in their winter home in Texas.

The Aransas refuge is threatened by another form of pollution because it is close to major traffic lanes for oil tankers and other tankers carrying benzene and other toxic materials. It is also close to oil- and gas-drilling operations. The presence of so many ships carrying oil in

▲ Whooping cranes face threats that include loss of habitat, disease, and dangerous obstacles such as power lines along their migratory path.

the Gulf of Mexico means that an oil spill off the coast of Texas is a real possibility. In other areas, oil spills have proven to be disastrous for wildlife. Because the wild flock of whooping cranes is still so small, an oil spill could destroy the entire flock. Some tankers have voluntarily changed their vessels to minimize the chance of spills, but the risk remains.

Power Lines

An increasing human demand for electricity has introduced another threat into the whoopers' environment. Power lines are an ever-present danger for whooping cranes. Today, more whooping cranes die from collisions with power lines than from gunshot wounds. Unfortunately, additional power lines were recently put up close to the Aransas refuge. People concerned with the cranes' welfare think there are simple ways to avoid power-line collisions: Colored balls could be placed on wires to help whooping cranes and other birds avoid crashing into them, for example.

Other Threats

Power lines are only one of the dangers that threaten whooping cranes on their long migration south from northern Canada to Texas. Conservationists believe that a hurricane along the route could wipe out the flock just as a hurricane destroyed the Louisiana flock.

The long migration also makes the cranes more vulnerable to predators. As wetlands disappear along the migration route, cranes rest in less-than-ideal situations. They choose to sleep on elevated places in water so that

▲ *Power lines continue to pose a threat to migrating whooping cranes.*

they are aware of predators in time to fly away or fight. Such accommodations are more and more difficult to find along the migration route. Conservationists estimate that only one in four chicks survives the long migration.

Disease is another threat. Each spring and autumn, more than 10 million ducks and geese, 500,000 sandhill cranes, and hundreds of other bird species as well as the wild whooping cranes congregate along an 80-mile-stretch of the Platte River in Nebraska. The presence of so many birds from so many places in a relatively small area (compared to the area available to migratory birds a century ago) increases the chance that birds might spread disease. Avian cholera, caused by a bacterium, is one disease that spreads easily when too many birds come together in one place.[11]

Funding

Since humans were responsible for pushing whooping cranes to the edge of extinction half a century ago, it is up to humans to ensure that whoopers continue to exist. Many people have been working to bring the species back to a sustainable number. Biologists, veterinarians, and other specialists work at research centers, studying the cranes as they incubate eggs and raise chicks. But these research facilities require money to operate. The programs that attempt to reintroduce cranes into the wild also require money. With so many competing demands on money from the federal government and money raised by nonprofit conservation groups, finding the funds to support whooping crane programs and facilities is a challenge.

PROTECTION

By 1973, the year that the United States Congress passed the Endangered Species Act (ESA), there were few whooping cranes left to protect. But the federal government had been taking steps to protect the whooping crane, both directly and indirectly, since the beginning of the twentieth century.

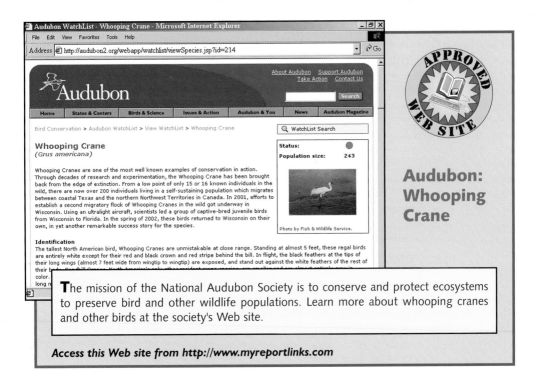

The mission of the National Audubon Society is to conserve and protect ecosystems to preserve bird and other wildlife populations. Learn more about whooping cranes and other birds at the society's Web site.

Access this Web site from http://www.myreportlinks.com

▶ Hats and Acts

The first federal legislation aimed at protecting wading birds, including cranes, came as the result of a trend in women's hats. In the 1880s, large hats adorned with birds' feathers were fashionable. Unfortunately, the demand for showy feathers, or plumes, continued into the next century, and "plume hunters" slaughtered adult birds as fast as they could. But not all women were happy with the practice. Two women from Massachusetts began a campaign in 1896 to get women to stop wearing hats adorned with bird feathers. Their work led to the founding of the first state Audubon Society in the United States, named after the noted American naturalist and bird artist John Jay Audubon.

Despite their efforts, large white birds, especially egrets and other wading birds, continued to disappear from the landscape. Finally in 1900, the federal government passed the Lacey Act. The Lacey Act, which was the "first attempt by any government anywhere to protect wildlife," made it illegal to ship birds and animals across state lines if those birds or animals were killed in violation of state laws.[1]

States had been passing laws to restrict hunting since the early 1700s. In 1710, New York instituted the first closed hunting season on birds.[2] However, state laws were rarely enforced. At first the Lacey Act, too, was little more than a gesture. The government employed fewer than half a dozen game wardens to enforce the law.

▶ The National Wildlife Refuge System

When Theodore "Teddy" Roosevelt became president of the United States in 1901, wildlife found a powerful friend. An outdoorsman and a man of action, Roosevelt pushed for tighter enforcement of the Lacey Act. But his most important contribution to the future of the country's wildlife was the establishment of more than fifty federal wildlife refuges. On March 14, 1903, Teddy Roosevelt signed the executive order that established the first federal bird reservation, which was on Pelican Island off the coast of Florida. The Pelican Island reservation, which later became a national wildlife refuge, marked the first time that the federal government set aside land for wildlife—yet the event hardly made news.

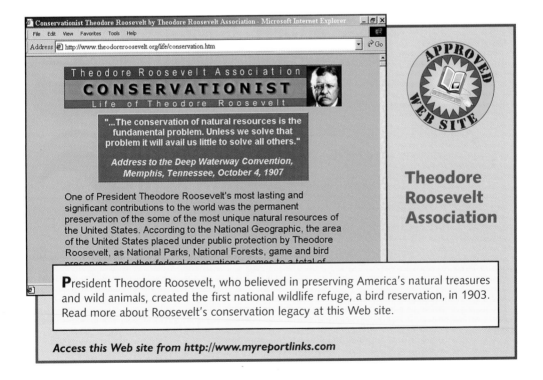

President Theodore Roosevelt, who believed in preserving America's natural treasures and wild animals, created the first national wildlife refuge, a bird reservation, in 1903. Read more about Roosevelt's conservation legacy at this Web site.

Access this Web site from http://www.myreportlinks.com

As one wildlife expert with the Smithsonian Institution has written, "There was no sense that this was the beginning of something that would produce immeasurable benefits for generations to come. . . . The refuge system is truly an American original. There is nothing else like it in the world."[3]

▶ Advances in Conservation

Roosevelt cared about wildlife, and he wanted others in government to care, too. In 1906, he required Congress, the Supreme Court, and the nation's governors to attend a conservation conference. In fact, the term *conservation* was coined by Roosevelt's forestry chief, Gifford Pinchot, who defined it as "the greatest good to the greatest number for the longest time."[4]

Despite these advances, plume hunters continued to slaughter birds. In 1913, Congress passed the Weeks-McLean Law, giving federal protection to birds migrating across state borders. But the Weeks-McLean Law was soon not considered strong enough and was replaced by the Migratory Bird Treaty Act of 1918. That act finally put an end to the commercial trade of birds and their feathers and helped bring the United States into international agreements to protect migratory birds.

In 1929, Congress passed the Migratory Bird Conservation Act, which included provisions for purchasing private land for bird refuges by establishing a Migratory Bird Conservation Commission.

When the Aransas National Wildlife Refuge was established in Texas in 1937, the whooping cranes' winter home was put under the protection of the federal government. By then, however, only about forty birds were alive to take advantage of the protection.

A Continuing Threat—and New Friends

While Congress worked to pass and enforce laws that would protect birds from people who made money by killing them in large numbers, another equally serious threat was not addressed. As farmers drained wetlands to grow crops, wading birds had fewer and fewer places to live.

In 1934, wading birds found an important friend in Roger Tory Peterson, who published *A Field Guide to the Birds,* which encouraged Americans to watch and value wild birds by offering simple techniques to identify bird

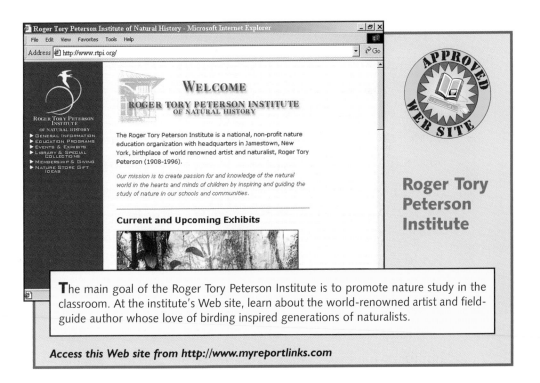

The main goal of the Roger Tory Peterson Institute is to promote nature study in the classroom. At the institute's Web site, learn about the world-renowned artist and field-guide author whose love of birding inspired generations of naturalists.

Access this Web site from http://www.myreportlinks.com

species. More and more bird-watchers began to care that such magnificent birds as whooping cranes and trumpeter swans were disappearing.

Whoopers and other wildlife found more protection in 1940 when the Bureau of Biological Survey and the Bureau of Fisheries, which had been moved to the Department of the Interior a year earlier, were combined to create the United States Fish and Wildlife Service (USFWS). The mission of the USFWS is to conserve and protect native fish, wildlife, and plant species. Today the USFWS maintains most of the protected wetlands in the country. These laws and the establishment of wildlife refuges gradually lessened the decline of whooping cranes and other wetland birds during the first half of the twentieth century.

▶ The IUCN

By the middle of the twentieth century, conservationists around the world were concerned about the rate at which species of all kinds were becoming extinct. In 1948, they came together to form the International Union for the Protection of Nature (IUPN). The organization changed its name in 1956 to the International Union for the Conservation of Nature and Natural Resources (IUCN). That name was shortened in 1990 to IUCN—The World Conservation Union.

One of IUCN's important contributions was categorizing species at risk into well-defined groups. For example, a species is critically endangered when its numbers have declined by at least 80 percent during

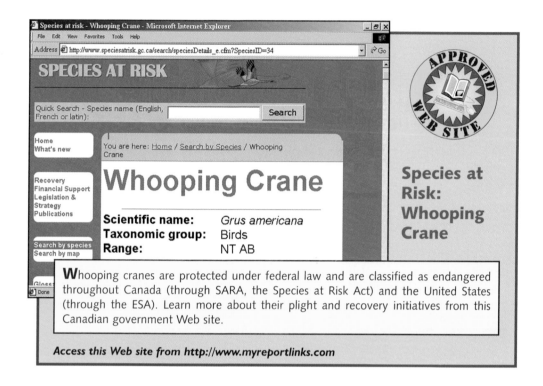

Species at Risk: Whooping Crane

Whooping Crane

Scientific name: *Grus americana*
Taxonomic group: Birds
Range: NT AB

Whooping cranes are protected under federal law and are classified as endangered throughout Canada (through SARA, the Species at Risk Act) and the United States (through the ESA). Learn more about their plight and recovery initiatives from this Canadian government Web site.

Access this Web site from http://www.myreportlinks.com

the past decade or three generations, and fewer than two hundred fifty full-grown individuals exist. These measurements helped people see more clearly what was happening to the wildlife around them.

Public Awareness in the United States

In the United States, too, people began to take action to save endangered species. In 1955, public protests prevented a U.S. Air Force bombing range from being extended into the whooping crane's winter home in Texas.[5] People became aware that they as well as endangered species are affected by an environment that cannot support wildlife. Their concerns prompted Congress to pass the Water Pollution Control Act in 1956. The National Environmental Policy Act followed in 1969.

This law requires federal agencies that are planning major projects to file environmental impact statements before construction can begin.

Important legislation came in 1972 when amendments to the Water Pollution Control Act (called the Clean Water Act) set national goals for cleaner bodies of water. The Clean Water Act protects navigable waters and adjoining shorelines from pollution.

▶ The Endangered Species Act

The 1960s brought the beginning of legislation to protect endangered species. Congress passed the Endangered

In the 1960s and 1970s, legislation to curb pollution and improve water quality also helped whooping cranes and other species to survive in North America. These whoopers, an adult and a juvenile, seen on the **International Crane Foundation** Web site, might not be around otherwise.

EDITOR'S CHOICE

Species Protection Act in 1966 and the Endangered Species Conservation Act in 1969. Neither legislation was strong enough to be very effective, however.

But in 1973, Congress passed the Endangered Species Act, which was a law that left no doubt about its determination to protect endangered species. Lawmakers as well as scientists had come to realize that people are part of a very complex environment that science does not yet fully understand. The great variety of plant and animal life offers "keys to puzzles which we cannot solve, and may provide answers to questions which we have not yet learned to ask," wrote the House Merchant Marine and Fisheries Committee in a document about the pressing need to protect endangered species.[6]

The drafters of the Endangered Species Act also recognized that we still have a lot to learn about the interdependence of various species and ecosystems. As a result, the ESA is probably one of the earliest examples of legislation that includes what is called the "precautionary principle."[7] In other words, the ESA assumes that actions should be taken to protect species even without scientific proof that those steps are necessary.

What the ESA Does

The Endangered Species Act includes a process for determining whether a plant or animal species should be added to the list of endangered plant and animal species. Endangered species are those considered in danger of becoming extinct, while threatened species are those considered likely to become endangered. The ESA also provides two important protections for listed plants and animals. First, the act makes it illegal for anyone to kill or harm an individual animal or plant of that species. Second, federal agencies must make sure that no federal funds or other federal laws have a negative impact on the continued existence of a listed species or the habitat critical to that species.

According to one conservationist, the ESA "has proven to be far ahead of its time by focusing not just on the conservation of all endangered and threatened plant and animal species, but more importantly on the conservation of 'the ecosystems upon which they depend.'"[8]

The ESA's Impact on Individuals

The ESA affects the actions of individuals as well as those of federal agencies. According to the act, individuals must not "take" a listed species, which means they may not "harass, harm, pursue, hunt, shoot, wound, kill, trap, capture, or collect, or attempt to engage in any such conduct."[9] Harming a listed species includes doing anything to the environment that might harm an individual plant or animal. For example, a farmer plowing his field might accidentally harm an endangered plant or animal.

Unfortunately, one little plant that a farmer might think of as a weed could suddenly bring the federal government into that farmer's backyard. While the farmer might think protecting endangered species is a great idea, he might strongly resent having the federal government tell him he cannot grow crops on certain

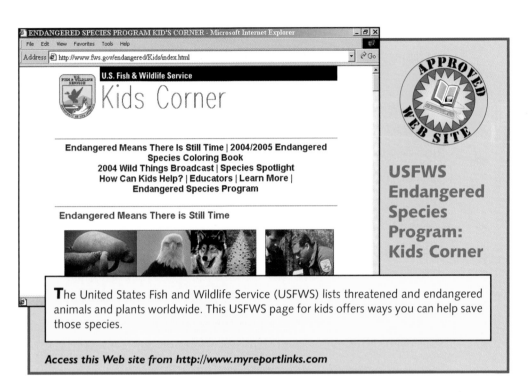

File Edit View Favorites Tools Help

Address http://www.fws.gov/endangered/Kids/index.html   Go

U.S. Fish & Wildlife Service

Kids Corner

Endangered Means There Is Still Time | 2004/2005 Endangered
Species Coloring Book
2004 Wild Things Broadcast | Species Spotlight
How Can Kids Help? | Educators | Learn More |
Endangered Species Program

Endangered Means There is Still Time

**USFWS
Endangered
Species
Program:
Kids Corner**

The United States Fish and Wildlife Service (USFWS) lists threatened and endangered animals and plants worldwide. This USFWS page for kids offers ways you can help save those species.

Access this Web site from http://www.myreportlinks.com

areas of his land. For the farmer, finding an endangered species on his land could be the beginning of a costly battle. Not being able to use land that is supposed to produce crops could be just the beginning. When the ESA was first passed, landowners feared that they would lose their land to the federal government.

The government attempted to lessen the act's impact by excusing private companies and individuals who might unintentionally harm a member of a listed species. But it still required private landowners, corporations, and state and local governments to develop a habitat conservation plan (HCP) when they made any changes to habitat that could harm a species on the list.[10] In most cases, people who were told they could not do what they wanted with their own land were still not happy.

Recently, the ESA has taken greater steps toward building partnerships with landowners and encouraging conservation of listed species on private land. The "no surprises" rule assures people that, even if the listed species on their land takes a turn for the worse, they will not be asked to do any more than they promised in their HCPs. Instead, the federal government will have to find another way to help that species.

The Endangered Species Act faces new opponents and new battles on a regular basis because it protects resources, usually in the forms of land and water, that people want to use. It is not always easy to keep the long-term benefit in mind when doing so means a short-term sacrifice. However, its continued focus on all we are losing is invaluable to the preservation of our world.

Chapter 5

SAVING THE WHOOPING CRANE

In 1967, researchers with the United States Fish and Wildlife Service and the Canadian Wildlife Service began taking "extra" eggs from whooping crane nests in Wood Buffalo National Park. Naturalists wanted to raise whooping crane chicks in other locations in case a disaster wiped out the lone wild flock. A hurricane or an oil spill in the cranes' winter residence at the Aransas National Wildlife Refuge, for example, could spell disaster for the cranes.

Because whooping cranes usually lay two eggs but raise only one chick, the naturalists decided they could increase the whooping crane population by taking one egg from each clutch of two, hatching the egg in an incubator, and raising the chick themselves. So, instead of hatching in a nest in northern Canada, chicks in the "borrowed" eggs hatched at the Patuxent Wildlife Research Center in Laurel, Maryland; the International Crane Foundation in Baraboo, Wisconsin; and the Calgary Zoo in Alberta, Canada.

▶ Hopes for a New Wild Flock

Raising chicks in captivity meant that survival of the species was not entirely dependent upon one wild flock.

But naturalists thought that an even better solution would be to have several wild flocks in addition to the captive cranes, and they came up with an idea. In 1976, they placed fourteen eggs from Wood Buffalo whooping crane nests in the nests of sandhill cranes at Grays Lake National Wildlife Refuge in southeast Idaho. Sandhill cranes, which are not endangered, are gray instead of white, and they do not grow as tall as whooping cranes. The two crane species are similar enough, though, that crane specialists hoped that the sandhill cranes would raise the whooping crane chicks. These foster parents could then teach the whooping crane chicks their

▲ A sandhill crane incubates a whooper egg at the Patuxent Wildlife Research Center. Although early attempts to have sandhills act as surrogate parents failed, these nonendangered cranes have proved useful in helping to restore the whooper population.

migration route from the Grays Lake refuge to the Bosque del Apache National Wildlife Refuge in New Mexico. This migration route, which covers about eight hundred miles (thirteen hundred kilometers), is much shorter and less dangerous than the trip from northern Canada to the coast of Texas.

Between 1975 and 1989, 380 whooping crane eggs were placed in sandhill crane nests. Those eggs produced eighty-five fledged whooping cranes.[1] The sandhill cranes proved to be good foster parents, and the young whoopers flew with them each fall and spring. The experiment seemed to be working well.

▶A Doomed Experiment

Several problems soon became evident, however. For one thing, whooping cranes were killed when they flew into power lines, which the smaller sandhill cranes avoided. Other whooping cranes contracted diseases, apparently from the large population of snow geese that shared the Bosque del Apache refuge.

The problem that doomed the experiment, though, was that the whooping cranes raised by sandhill cranes did not realize that they *were* whooping cranes, and so they could not find mates. The whooping crane flock produced no eggs. The sandhill cranes succeeded in teaching their foster chicks how to find food and follow their migration route, but they could not teach the young whoopers how to attract mates of their own kind. The experimental program ended in 1989. For years, this flock of whooping cranes continued to migrate between Idaho and New Mexico, but no whooping crane chicks were born to replace the adults that died. Unfortunately, the last surviving Grays Lake whooping crane died in 2003.

Another Experiment

A few years after the sandhill cranes hatched the first whooper foster chicks, crane researchers began to think aloud about establishing a flock that would live in Florida year-round and would not migrate north in the spring. The birds in a nonmigratory flock would not need foster parents to teach them a migration route.

Five years later, in 1984, the USFWS began to consider potential areas for a nonmigratory flock of whooping cranes. It decided that the flock would be

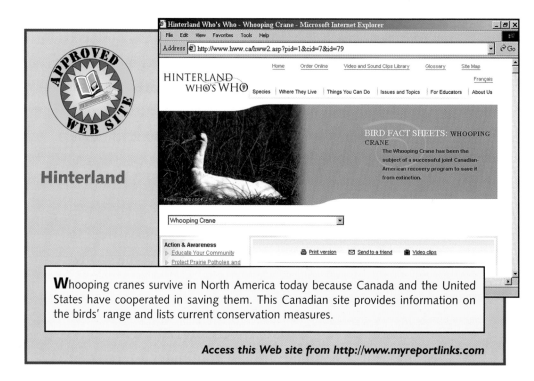

Whooping cranes survive in North America today because Canada and the United States have cooperated in saving them. This Canadian site provides information on the birds' range and lists current conservation measures.

Access this Web site from http://www.myreportlinks.com

considered a "nonessential experimental population," using a designation allowed by Section 10 of the Endangered Species Act.[2] An experimental population is considered threatened rather than endangered. By classifying the proposed flock as experimental, USFWS officials provided more flexibility in developing the program. The designation also meant that the program would be less threatening to local citizens. The potential for any restrictions on private activities was further reduced because the new flock would also be considered "nonessential to the continued existence of the species."[3]

Choosing a Location

For three years, the Whooping Crane Recovery Team, made up of American and Canadian wildlife officials, studied possible release sites. By 1988, the team had decided to release the whooping cranes in Florida's Kissimmee prairies, which is an area of shallow lakes and palmetto scrub. It is home to few humans but plenty of Florida sandhill cranes that do not migrate.[4] The recovery team submitted the proposal for public comment, and the location was approved.

The recovery team then decided on one more study. The specialists wanted to know if the "children" of the wild, migrating whooping cranes would be born with the migrating instinct. Would the young whoopers they released in Florida decide to leave on their own in the spring? To find out, researchers took eggs from the nests of a migratory flock of sandhill cranes and put those eggs in twenty-three nests belonging to nonmigrating sandhill cranes. When the foster chicks did not migrate in the fall, the scientists concluded that the migrating instinct in cranes needs to be "triggered" by parents. (Experiments of this kind are done with sandhill cranes because they are not endangered.)

Raising "Wild" Whoopers

The next step was to raise whooper chicks suited for release in the wild. These chicks would need to see people not as friends but as enemies. The International Crane Foundation developed a method of rearing the chicks by making their human handlers dress in costumes. The costume itself is very strange and, to human eyes, looks nothing like a crane. It is simply a white hood and mantle. The costume wearer holds a puppet that features a cranelike neck, head, and bill. The costume disguises the human form, and costume-reared chicks are prevented from seeing or hearing people at all, except in stressful situations.

First Arrivals

In January 1993, the first cohort of young whoopers from the International Crane Foundation and Patuxent arrived at their new home in Florida. All were six to eight months old, an age when cranes tend not to fight one another once the hierarchy in the cohort is established. For a month, the cranes were kept in a large pen, and they wore harnesses called brails that keep one wing at a time from fully extending so that the cranes cannot fly. By keeping the cranes in one place with plenty of food,

△ The "adult whooper" teaching this chick to feed is actually a lifelike whooper puppet worn by a costumed handler.

researchers hoped to establish "place loyalty" so that the cranes would not wander too far when they were released. Unfortunately, the pen, which was placed close to the water, was soon left high and dry by drought.

That first winter, the results of the experiment were discouraging. Bobcats soon killed five of the young whoopers because the cranes had not learned to roost in open water. Wild whooping cranes sleep on elevated land (a sandbar, for example) in water that is more than

▲ Bobcats pose a threat to young whooping cranes who have not yet learned to roost in safe places, like open water.

8 inches (20 centimeters) deep. The young cranes were accustomed to pens, and they hid in reeds and bushes where, if they had been raised in the wild, their parents would never have led them.[5]

Naturalists had hoped that the young whooping cranes would imitate the sandhill cranes around them so they could learn where to find food and how to avoid danger. Instead, the young whoopers called to other white birds, such as great egrets, white pelicans, and white ibis. When the sandhill cranes flew overhead in the early evening, heading for safe places to spend the night, the young whoopers continued to forage—and became easy prey for bobcats. (Bobcats had increased in number in the region because their natural predators had disappeared from the environment.)

Of the fourteen cranes released in 1993, only five survived the first year. More whoopers were released in 1994, but bobcats continued to kill the precious few young whooping cranes.

Back to the Drawing Board

While Florida researchers trapped bobcats and removed them from the area, researchers at the International Crane Foundation and Patuxent added new "classes" to the whooping cranes' education. Water was included in the rearing pens, and the costumed caretakers led the young cranes into the water to roost at night.

New release pens were made of plastic fencing instead of steel so that they could be moved if the water dried up. One end of the pen was placed in the water to encourage whoopers to roost there at night. The scientists also found new release sites. The best release sites turned out to be located on private property. Fortunately, local landowners cooperated with the program and allowed the cranes to be released on their land.

In 1995 and 1996, sixty-four whoopers were released on six privately owned sites, and 70 percent of those whoopers survived the first year. The program seemed to turn a corner.

The program's goal, however, was not simply to ship young whooping cranes to Florida. The goal was to have a self-sustaining flock. In other words, the cranes needed

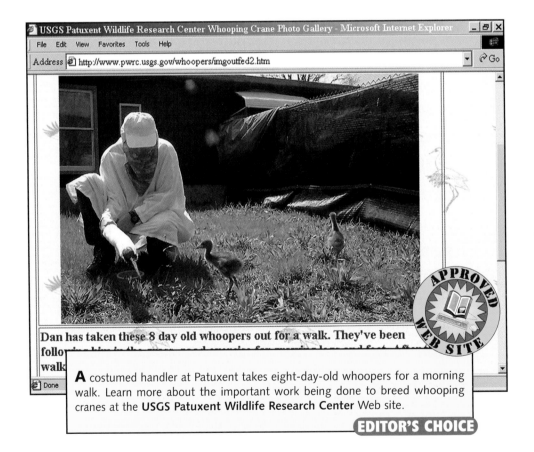

USGS Patuxent Wildlife Research Center Whooping Crane Photo Gallery - Microsoft Internet Explorer

File   Edit   View   Favorites   Tools   Help

Address   http://www.pwrc.usgs.gov/whoopers/imgoutfed2.htm

Dan has taken these 8 day old whoopers out for a walk. They've been
follo
walk

A costumed handler at Patuxent takes eight-day-old whoopers for a morning walk. Learn more about the important work being done to breed whooping cranes at the **USGS Patuxent Wildlife Research Center** Web site.

EDITOR'S CHOICE

to reproduce. The question remained, Could whooping cranes raised in captivity by costumed "parents" become parents on their own?

An exciting development came in 1997. By then, the survivors of the first cohort were mature, and researchers saw a pair preparing to start a family. They had driven sandhill cranes from an area they claimed as their own territory, and they were building nests on the edge of a lake. The pair did not lay eggs, though, and in June the male disappeared. The next year, researchers saw more pairs and more nests, but no eggs. They believed that three years of drought in Florida may have affected the cranes' ability to lay eggs.

Then in 1999, two pairs produced eggs. Unfortunately, neither clutch produced a chick. A predator took the eggs in one nest, while the other two eggs were lost in flooding after heavy rains. Nearly two hundred whooping cranes had been released, and the program had not resulted in a single chick.

▶ A Bright Spot on the Horizon

Finally, in March of 2000, seven years into the experimental program, the first wild whooping crane to be born in the United States in sixty years kicked its way out of its egg. The chick lived about seventy days before a bobcat caught it, but its birth showed that the program could work. According to a researcher who had championed the program from the beginning, the chick and its parents proved that "these birds, raised in captivity and with little or no natural experience, can get it right.

Everything we saw from this pair suggests that they were doing everything they were supposed to do."[6]

Lucky

Two years later, in March 2002, a chick named Lucky hatched and grew up to become the first bird to be produced by captive-reared, wild-released parents that reached fledging age. Lucky was soon followed by another chick. The fact that seventeen nesting attempts in three years produced only two fledged young whoopers by 2002 illustrates how much time it takes for whooping cranes to increase their numbers.

By 2004, researchers thought they were finally justified in believing that a new wild whooping crane flock could survive in Florida. Two more chicks, one who was Lucky's sister, fledged in the wild. Another chick born in 2004 survived the dangerous developmental stage when whoopers cannot yet fly. But even though drought conditions subsided, and more pairs built nests, all of the chicks were killed by predators. Still, researchers are hopeful that the goal of the program—twenty-five pairs of nonmigratory cranes reproducing at a self-sustaining rate—will be met even though only about 37 percent of the nonmigratory flock has survived.

The Second New Wild Flock

The United States Fish and Wildlife Service's recovery plan for the whooping crane calls for not one but two wild, geographically separate flocks of twenty-five nesting pairs. When the Florida nonmigratory flock started to show signs of success, crane specialists began to imagine a new flock that could be taught to migrate.

Just a few years earlier, such an idea would have seemed impossible. Cranes need to learn migration routes. The Grays Lake attempt to have sandhills teach whoopers a new migration route had proved unsuccessful. The whoopers learned the route, but they did not become self-sustaining.

But what if humans could teach young whooping cranes how to be whooping cranes? And what if humans could teach them where to migrate? The work done at the International Crane Foundation and the Patuxent

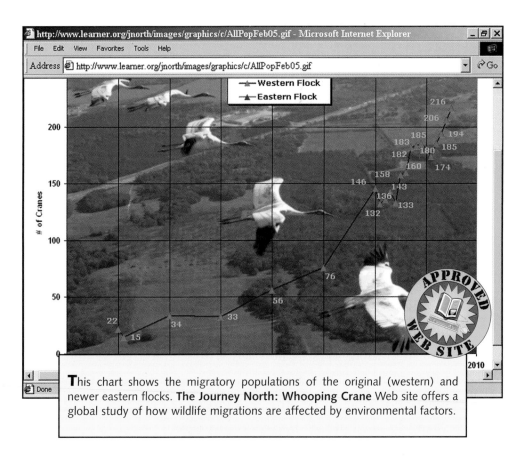

This chart shows the migratory populations of the original (western) and newer eastern flocks. **The Journey North: Whooping Crane** Web site offers a global study of how wildlife migrations are affected by environmental factors.

Wildlife Research Center preparing young whooping cranes for life in the wild in Florida proved that humans could raise whooper chicks that would grow up to be successful parents. And with imagination and determination, one man proved that humans could teach birds to migrate.

▶ Operation Migration

William Lishman, a Canadian artist, was already an ultralight pilot when he saw a movie about Canada geese who followed a boat. He thought that if geese could follow a boat, surely they could follow an ultralight aircraft. He enlisted the help of the film's animal trainer, Bill Carrick, and began working with Canada geese, which are not endangered. In 1993, Lishman and a partner, Joseph Duff, taught eighteen geese to migrate from Ontario, Canada, to Virginia.[7] Most important, the geese flew home by themselves the following spring. If Canada geese could be taught to migrate, perhaps whooping cranes could be, too.

The following year, the two established Operation Migration Inc. to help conserve endangered migratory species. Incorporated as a Canadian charitable organization, Operation Migration seeks to promote conservation through research, education, and the formation of partnerships. Its technique of using ultralight aircraft to guide bird migrations was again used with Canada geese and sandhill cranes before it was approved for use with whooping cranes by the Whooping Crane Recovery Team. In September 1999, Operation Migration joined with eight other groups (some government funded and some nonprofit) to form the Whooping Crane Eastern Partnership. The partnership's mission was to carry out the reintroduction of the eastern migratory flock.

Experimentation With Another Species

Because whooping cranes are critically endangered, conservationists try new ideas on sandhill cranes when they

▲ Cranes that are part of the 2004 eastern migration follow pilot Joe Duff of Operation Migration as they near their destination, the Chassahowitzka National Wildlife Refuge in Florida.

can. So, in the spring of 2000, sandhill crane eggs at the Patuxent Wildlife Research Center were exposed to the sounds of an ultralight engine during the final ten days of incubation. Before they were even two weeks old, the sandhill crane chicks, working with silent costumed trainers, began exercising every day with an ultralight. When they were older, the chicks boarded an aircraft headed for the Necedah National Wildlife Refuge in Wisconsin. They continued their training there each day and soon learned to fly with the ultralight.

On October 3, 2000, three ultralights with a cohort of eleven sandhill fledglings began the migration to the

In this photo from **Operation Migration,** a whooper that is spending the fall and winter in Florida is coaxed into its pen by a costumed handler.

EDITOR'S CHOICE

Chassahowitzka National Wildlife Refuge in Florida. The journey took forty days and required the assistance of many property owners along the way, but the chicks arrived safely in Florida. The real proof of the experiment's success came six months later. In the spring of 2001, the sandhill cranes migrated back to Wisconsin by themselves, returning to the exact spot where they had begun their migration the previous fall.

Whooper Pioneers

At Patuxent, handlers began exposing whooper eggs to the sound of an ultralight engine in the spring of 2001. One difference between the whoopers and the sandhill cranes became apparent as soon as the young chicks were exposed to the ultralight. When sandhill cranes were frightened, they ran for cover in the weeds and had to be rounded up. When the whooper chicks were frightened, they stayed closer to the costumed "parent." Later, the crane handlers noticed that the young whoopers had learned to identify the ultralight as the parent. When fledgling cranes became confused or frightened, they wanted to be close to the flying machine.

On July 10, 2001, ten young whoopers arrived at the Necedah refuge for their flight training. One of the ten chicks died, and another was sent to the Audubon Zoo in New Orleans when trainers decided she would not be able to make the long flight. But eight fledglings were able to complete flight training.

The first ultralight-led whooper migration was not as easy as the previous year's sandhill crane migration.

From the beginning, unfavorable weather caused delays. Finally, on October 17, three days after the proposed departure date, the eight whoopers and a fourteen-person team began the migration. In addition to four pilots, a ten-member support team drove from one stopover point to the next to set up pens and help care for the cranes.

For the next fifty days, every morning began with a flurry of activity as the team evaluated flight conditions, sometimes taking an early morning test flight. Fog, rain, or choppy winds meant the next leg of the trip would need to be delayed. In all, the cranes and their support team spent twenty-four of the fifty days on the ground.

One week into the migration, tragedy struck. High winds caused the cranes' portable pen to collapse. When two members of the crew went to check on the cranes late in the evening, they were gone. During the next four hours, until two in the morning, the crew located and rounded up seven of the young cranes. The next morning they found the eighth crane. It had collided with a power line and was dead.

▶ Tense Moments in the Skies

Even when the weather was good, flying with the cranes brought tense moments for the pilots. As pilot Joseph Duff explained, the young whooping cranes usually fly in a consistent order, but the more dominant whoopers compete for leadership. Since they see the ultralight as another crane, more aggressive young whoopers would occasionally challenge it for the lead position. Suddenly, just when everything seemed perfect, according to Duff, a whooper would "move from a perfectly comfortable spot only inches from the wing-tip," where he could fly effortlessly in the wake of the aircraft, and drop under the wing. Duff described the scene around him: "You can almost see the determination in his [the crane's] eye as he pumps past and moves in front of the aircraft. Each bird follows the one ahead and soon the space around the aircraft is an obstacle course of white feathers on seven-foot wings."[8]

Weather delays were not the only problems. In October and November 2001, heightened security after

The cranes and Brooke upon arrival in Morgan County, IN.

An ultralight pilot with **Operation Migration** and the whoopers following him land at a stopover in Indiana during the fall migration south.

EDITOR'S CHOICE

the September 11 terrorist attacks on the World Trade Center in New York City and the Pentagon outside Washington, D.C., required pilots to detour to avoid flying within ten miles of nuclear power plants. Approval to fly close to a control zone was usually followed by many questions about the migration. Another problem surfaced when one crane would not follow the ultralight consistently, and he distracted other whoopers. In the end, caretakers wound up taking him from one stop to another by truck.

A Successful Migration

Finally, on December 5, after twenty-six days of flying from 20 to 94 miles (32 to 151 kilometers) in a day, the seven young whoopers arrived at the Chassahowitzka refuge in Florida.

Shortly after arriving in Florida, two of the first migrating class were killed by bobcats, but the remaining five whoopers made themselves at home in their sunny new surroundings and were able to survive the winter. Then, on April 9 of the following spring, they left for the long flight back to Wisconsin. Four of the whoopers made the flight in only ten days and landed within a quarter mile of their training site. Radio and satellite transmitters on their legs allowed researchers with the Whooping Crane Eastern Partnership to track them—and watch in amazement as the young birds averaged more than 200 miles (322 kilometers) a day.

Left on their own, four of the whoopers cut 50 miles (81 kilometers) from the migration route by flying

NATURE. Flight School | PBS - Microsoft Internet Explorer

File Edit View Favorites Tools Help

Address http://www.pbs.org/wnet/nature/flightschool/ Go

NATURE ::NATURE Home ::Current Season ::Episode Index ::NATURE Shop ::Contact Us ::For Teachers

VIDEO Database | PUZZLES & Fun | EPISODE Previews | CRITTER Guide

Flight School

Whooping cranes learn survival lessons from human surrogate parents on NATURE's FLIGHT SCHOOL.

At five-feet tall, with a wing span of nearly eight feet, whooping cranes are among the largest and most beautiful birds of North America. But hunting and other forms of human encroachment drove them to the very edge of extinction in the mid-20th century, when the head count for the last known flock plummeted to an all-time low of just 15. Legal protection, conservation measures, and

VIDEO

SPECIAL FEATURES

Flyways
Discover the superhighways of the sky.
●●●●●

Imprinting
Learn about the man who walked with geese.

Flight School

This PBS site tells the story of the long and dangerous journey from Wisconsin to Florida that helped establish the eastern migratory population of whooping cranes.

Access this Web site from http://www.myreportlinks.com

directly over large cities that the ultralight had to avoid. The fifth whooper, a female, took off on her own over Tennessee. Flying by herself, she arrived in Wisconsin two weeks later than the rest of her cohort.

Seven whooping cranes and fourteen people proved that humans could teach whoopers to migrate. Each year since 2001, a cohort of young whooping cranes follows ultralight aircraft to Florida, and each spring they return to Wisconsin. Lessons learned as naturalists released nonmigratory whoopers in Florida have benefited the migratory flock. In March 2005, about 85 percent of the cranes had survived; the migrating flock totaled forty-five whooping cranes.

Free Photos - ICF - Microsoft Internet Explorer

File   Edit   View   Favorites   Tools   Help

Address http://www.savingcranes.org/photo/free/photo.cfm?p=94   Go

This photograph of a wading whooper, found in the **International Crane Foundation** Web site's gallery, can be downloaded to use in a report on whooping cranes.

EDITOR'S CHOICE

Each year the eastern migratory flock includes more experienced navigators, cranes that can travel the migratory route more quickly and often leave their summer home later in the fall. In 2004, crane trainers learned that the experienced cranes can be teachers.

One juvenile whooper, scheduled to follow an ultralight to Florida, developed feather problems. Feathers that developed abnormally had to be removed. By the time the new feathers grew in, the fledgling had missed too much training to be sent off with his cohort. Instead, he was released into a group of older cranes and followed them to Florida.

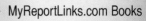
RAISING WILD WHOOPING CRANES

The decision to raise whooping cranes in captivity required a huge commitment of time and money. In the wild, raising one chick is a full-time job for two parents. But even today, after decades of raising whooping cranes in captivity, there are not enough whooping crane pairs to hatch and raise all the eggs. So it is up to people to raise, or hand-rear, most of the chicks. Chicks raised in captivity by whooping crane parents are referred to as "parent-reared chicks."

Without these captive-breeding programs, the reintroduction of wild whooping cranes would not have been possible. It is only after years of work by many dedicated people—and large amounts of money raised to fund that work—that whooping cranes are again flying in areas where the species had not been seen for more than a century.

Little was known about whooping cranes when biologists at the Patuxent Wildlife Research Center and the International Crane Foundation began raising whooper chicks. The researchers learned by trial and error. And that learning continues, adding to the species' chances of survival.

▶ Just the Right Facilities

Whooping crane chicks need more than a big fenced yard and a little house to sleep in. Facilities for hand-rearing chicks include brooder boxes and incubators for the eggs. They need indoor and outdoor pens large enough to allow chicks to get plenty of exercise. Indoor pens need to have heat lamps to control the temperature. Outdoor pens need a cover of netting or wire to keep out predators, such as eagles, and to keep the chicks contained when they learn to fly.

Researchers soon learned that the pens cannot have just any old floor. The legs are the most vulnerable part of whooping crane chicks because they grow so rapidly. And hand-reared chicks develop leg problems much more frequently than parent-reared chicks. According to wildlife experts, cranes can adapt to life in captivity with an injured wing, but if their undeveloped legs are injured, the injury can become life threatening very rapidly.[1] Researchers are looking at everything—from the nutrients in the food to how much exercise the chicks get—to find out why hand-reared chicks develop more leg problems.

Chicks raised in the wild learn to walk on soft marshy land. Researchers realized that a floor that is too slippery or too hard can cause deformities in the birds' long legs. The challenge has been to provide a floor that feels similar to marshy land but can be kept clean. Caretakers tried using about two inches of sand or wood shavings on the floor, but chicks often got those materials in their eyes and developed eye

This whooping crane, part of the wild flock that migrates from Canada to Texas, was shot as it flew over Kansas. Thanks to the efforts of veterinarians at Kansas State University and Patuxent, where it is now being cared for, this injured whooper may one day be returned to the wild.

problems. Then they tried indoor-outdoor carpet on top of the sand or shavings, and that combination seemed to provide a safe surface.[2]

Couch-Potato Chicks

Researchers also realized that another reason hand-reared chicks developed more leg problems than chicks raised by parents is that parent-reared chicks followed their parents all day and got plenty of exercise.

Caretakers do as much as they can to give hand-reared chicks lots of exercise. They take chicks for walks in an exercise yard and for swims in a swimming pool. But their human caretakers do not have the time to keep the chicks moving all day. Left on their own, chicks can be lazy. Caretakers soon learned that chicks placed in pens next to adult whooping cranes were much more active, and to their delight, both male and female whooping cranes showed an interest in the chicks, "talking" to them and even feeding them through the fence. Chicks can also be encouraged to get more exercise if insects and toys are added to their environment.

Aggression

What adds to the difficulty and expense of raising whooper chicks is the need to keep very young chicks separate. This must be done because they become aggressive toward one another, even when they are together for a short time.[3] (In the wild, only the stronger of the two chicks in a nest will survive.) At the same time, chicks need to see other cranes to know what they are. Ideally, brooder boxes, incubators, and indoor and

▲ Whooper chicks raised in captivity never see the human face or form of their costumed handlers, like this one from Patuxent. The disguise is used to prevent the whooper chicks from imprinting on humans, or forming a bond with them.

outdoor pens should be separated by sheets of clear acrylic plastic, which allow the chicks to see other chicks and models of adult cranes while preventing injuries from aggressive behavior.[4]

Veterinary Care

Facilities for the crane chicks must also provide veterinary care. Each new chick is precious to the people who work at the captive breeding facilities, and they do all they can to help each one survive. In addition to checking for parasites and infectious diseases, veterinarians occasionally have to perform surgery. Whooping cranes are attracted to shiny things and may swallow metal objects, which sometimes have to be removed surgically.

Important Lessons

Even the most basic behaviors, like eating and drinking, are not instinctive for whooper chicks. They need to be taught how to do these things by their parents. Newly hatched chicks, attracted to their parents' long bills, will watch the motion of the bills and peck at them. Since whooper parents teach their young by repeating motions with their bills, again and again, caretakers must do the same.

Crane chicks are attracted to the color red as well as to the long, thin shape of the adult crane's bill. So, when teaching the chicks how to eat and drink, caretakers have attached red objects to the bill of a puppet crane head or a syringe. The lesson begins with the caretakers playing a digital recording of a brood call on an MP3 player. Then the caretaker will place the tip of the puppet's bill

This newly hatched chick nestles up to its "mother," a puppet resembling an adult whooper. Learn more about captive-breeding efforts at the **Whooping Crane Eastern Partnership** Web site.

EDITOR'S CHOICE

in water before dipping it in the dry crumbs that make up the crane chow.[5] Even newly hatched chicks will usually peck at what they see as a parent's bill. Sooner or later, they will get crumbs on their own beaks and swallow the food.

Then, the handler can take the puppet and suspend it from the ceiling and tie part of it to a wall of the pen. That way, the puppet can purr and "bob" without the handler having to go into the pen.[6] After four to fourteen days of training, chicks will start eating on their own.

A similar technique can be used to teach chicks to drink, although it often takes a combination of techniques over several days before the chick is observed drinking on its own. One method is to use the puppet head to lure the chick to the water and then dip and drip the way that whooper parents do. The caretaker might use the puppet head to stir the water to attract the chick. Placing shiny objects in the water bowl might also attract the chick's attention. Another technique is to let water drip into the water bowl from a height of several inches. Many chicks will investigate the moving water and get a drink that way.[7]

Imprinting

Another important lesson that whooping crane chicks bred in captivity need to learn is that they *are* whooping cranes. Chicks born in the wild see their parents and begin imitating them. This instinct to imitate parents is called imprinting. But chicks who see humans before they see their own species may falsely imprint on people. So wildlife experts use imprinting models to help these whooper chicks identify themselves as whooping cranes. These models include stuffed whooping cranes and pelt fragments of crane feathers for cuddling as well as windows that allow chicks to see adult whooping cranes.

As chicks grow, they can be brought together in small groups of two or three for exercise. But, since whooper chicks are naturally aggressive and can even kill other chicks with their sharp beaks, they need to be carefully watched. They become less aggressive the closer they come to fledging. The fledglings in the cohort will quickly establish a dominance hierarchy. This social order, in which certain cranes will be dominant over others, allows the whoopers in the cohort to get along with each other.

Costumed "Parents" Teach Chicks How to Be Wild

When researchers decided to release young whoopers into the wild, it became even more challenging to raise

▲ A handler and ultralight pilot at the Necedah National Wildlife Refuge in Wisconsin train whooper chicks to think of the craft as a dominant crane.

whooper chicks. If they were going to survive in the wild, the whooping crane chicks would need to be raised so that they would have a natural fear of people and an attraction to their own kind.

To do this, researchers developed a method called costume-rearing. Caretakers don body-length white costumes that feature a loose hood and poncho. This costume disguises their human form beneath. At the end of one sleeve is a crane puppet that looks remarkably like a real whooper. The puppet is used to teach the chicks crane behaviors, such as poking at the ground to find insects.

Costume-rearing begins ten days before an egg hatches. At that time, human voices are no longer permitted in the incubator room. Digital recordings of crane brood calls are played at regular intervals, along with the sound of the ultralight aircraft engine, but not too often. (Playing the brood calls too often can stimulate the chick to hatch too early.)

For nearly all contact between caretakers and chicks, the caretaker wears a white costume to make it seem as much like an adult crane as possible. During a medical exam, when the chicks may naturally feel fear during the procedure, the caretaker wears a dark gray costume.

Survival Training

When the first young whoopers were released in Florida, researchers realized that an important part of their training had been neglected. The young whoopers had not learned to roost in water.

The Patuxent refuge raises chicks in dry pens because it is easier to keep them clean and ensure that disease does not break out. But researchers realized that the birds had to become more familiar with the environment they would find in Florida, so they constructed a marshy pond area. When chicks are very young, costumed caretakers lead them to the pond and help them explore it, much the way whooping crane parents would. When the young whoopers are seventy days old and are put together in cohorts, they are moved to a large pen with a pond. Caretakers help them explore the pond and learn to stand in the water. Cameras in the pen allow

USGS Patuxent Wildlife Research Center Whooping Crane Photo Gallery - Microsoft Internet Explorer

File   Edit   View   Favorites   Tools   Help

Address   http://www.pwrc.usgs.gov/whoopers/img81.htm   Go

Brenda shows a two week old whooper the wonders of the natural world when she brings him to a small pond. Using the puppet, she'll show him how to probe in the wet ground as he discovers how much fun a puddle can be. Frogs, earthworms, and flying insects are all there to tempt the young whooping Wildli

A two-week-old whooper raised at the **USGS Patuxent Wildlife Research Center** is introduced to a pond and all its interesting critters by one of the center's costumed handlers.

EDITOR'S CHOICE

researchers to see whether the cranes roost in water at night.

Preparation for Migration

Teaching young whooping cranes to fly behind an ultra-light aircraft requires additional training. The lessons begin even before the chicks hatch as caretakers play recordings of the ultralight engine and crane brooding calls. When the chicks are a few days old, costumed caretakers lead them to the ultralight so they become familiar with it. Again, the young chicks hear the ultralight and recorded crane brooding calls.

Soon a costumed pilot uses the ultralight to lead the young chicks on walks. By the time they are able to fly, the young whooping cranes have come to see the ultra-light as a dominant crane.

More to Learn

Researchers continue to look for answers that might help whooping cranes survive. For example, some whooping crane families seem to be more likely than others to sur-vive in the wild, and researchers are trying to figure out why. Other research projects include techniques for mon-itoring populations in the wild, lessons that will help young whoopers survive after release, ways to improve the health of whooping cranes in the wild, and better understanding of their genetic structure.[8]

THE FUTURE OF WHOOPING CRANES

The wild whooping crane population has increased from about fifteen individuals in 1941 to 328 at the end of 2004. That population increase is a testimony to what people can do to help an endangered species. Individuals, nonprofit organizations, and the United States Fish and Wildlife Service have all contributed money, time, and creativity to help America's tallest bird survive.

While the increase in numbers is promising, the future of the whooping crane remains uncertain. One threat in particular—habitat destruction—is still an unresolved problem. As the human population increases, maintaining habitat where whooping cranes can live and where they can rest during migration will become more challenging.

▶ A Growing Population

By the end of 2004, the Florida nonmigratory flock population had increased to sixty-nine, including fifteen nesting pairs. This flock is more than halfway to the goal of twenty-five nesting pairs. The new migratory flock has been very successful, although nesting pairs were just beginning to form by the end of 2004.

▲ The future of whooping cranes looks promising—but only if we continue to help them in their fight for survival.

At Patuxent, the International Crane Foundation, the San Antonio Zoo, and the Calgary Zoo in Canada, 29 nesting pairs, in a total population of 109 captive whooping cranes, continue to produce eggs for reintroduction programs.

Friends of the Cranes

Fortunately, whooping cranes have many friends, including individuals who volunteer time and resources to help them. The Whooping Crane Conservation Association (WCCA) had its beginnings in the 1950s as a small group of pen pals who formed the "Whooper Club." It was the first private organization to focus on the recovery of whooping cranes. It also proved that a small group of people *can* make a difference when it comes to saving species. These courageous few people were able to pressure the governments of both the United States and Canada to take action to save whooping cranes. And they did this while going against more established environmental organizations whose beliefs were that the species should be allowed to go extinct naturally. In 1961, the Whooper Club became the Whooping Crane Conservation Association and five years later became a nonprofit

The Whooping Crane Conservation Association began as a group of individuals who were concerned in the 1950s that this North American species would soon go extinct. Learn about the association's efforts to save cranes at the WCCA Web site.

EDITOR'S CHOICE

Access this Web site from http://www.myreportlinks.com

organization. Some of its members have since been instrumental in the captive-rearing programs now used at Patuxent.

The WCEP

The Whooping Crane Eastern Partnership includes the International Crane Foundation, Operation Migration Inc., the Wisconsin Department of Natural Resources, the United States Fish and Wildlife Service, the Patuxent Wildlife Research Center, the National Fish and Wildlife Foundation, the Natural Resources Foundation of Wisconsin, and the International Whooping Crane Recovery Team. In addition, many "flyway" states, Canadian provinces, private individuals, and conservation groups have contributed support to the project. Private sources in the form of grants, donations, and corporate sponsors have contributed more than 60 percent of the project's estimated $1.8 million budget.[1]

However, establishing a new wild migrating flock would not be possible without the help of people who host the whooping cranes and the team that travels with them. Each year, from twenty to thirty landowners open their homes to the migration team, providing them a place to stay and food to eat for as long as it takes to get the cranes from one stopover to another.

"The first juggling is to guess how much food you'll need to feed the fifteen to twenty crew members," explained one of the landowners helping the team. "The first year we expected an overnight stay, a couple of meals, and they'd be gone. Four days later, we'd exhausted our freezer, our imagination and nearby restaurants, awaiting a new propeller."[2]

▶ Supporting Players

Other friends are the nonprofit organizations, including the Nature Conservancy, that work to protect and preserve wetlands. The Nature Conservancy has begun to buy more than 50 million dollars' worth of wetlands.[3] Some of this land is donated by large corporations.

Whooping cranes also have friends in state and federal government agencies trying to protect endangered species and the National Wildlife Refuge system. The United States Fish and Wildlife Service, the National Park Service, and various state and local agencies have used tax dollars to purchase and protect wetlands.

One of the member organizations in the Whooping Crane Eastern Partnership, the Natural Resources Foundation of Wisconsin has helped reintroduce whooping cranes in Wisconsin. Visit the foundation's site to find out about its work.

Access this Web site from http://www.myreportlinks.com

▶ Protecting Our Wetlands

Perhaps the most important factor in ensuring the survival of whooping cranes and their wetlands habitat is the realization that people need healthy wetlands too. Wetlands are a vital part of the natural system that produces clean and reliable water supplies.

However, huge amounts of the country's wetlands are still not protected, and those lands continue to disappear. Some conservationists have predicted that all unprotected wetlands in the United States may be destroyed by the middle of this century.[4] Even protected wetlands are disappearing.

In Louisiana, for example, 51 percent of the Delta National Wildlife Refuge has disappeared into the Gulf of Mexico. Hurricanes and rising sea levels have claimed some of the refuge area, but the many changes made by humans—especially the Army Corps of Engineers—have hastened that disappearance. The delta was formed when rivers carrying a great deal of sediment ran freely into the gulf. Today, dams and reservoirs along the Mississippi River prevent the sediment from ever reaching the Delta National Wildlife Refuge. In addition, people have built canals for transportation and oil development. These canals allow water from the Gulf of Mexico to intrude deep into the delta and cause erosion.

In many other parts of the country, changes to lands that border national wildlife refuges are destroying the habitat inside those protected areas. Because wetlands depend on water and because the water comes from rivers

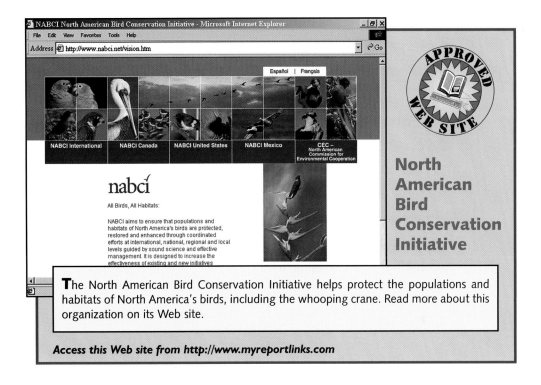

NABCI North American Bird Conservation Initiative - Microsoft Internet Explorer

File   Edit   View   Favorites   Tools   Help

Address http://www.nabci.net/vision.htm

Español | Français

NABCI International   NABCI Canada   NABCI United States   NABCI Mexico   CEC –
                                                                            North American
                                                                            Commission for
                                                                            Environmental Cooperation

nabci

All Birds, All Habitats:

NABCI aims to ensure that populations and habitats of North America's birds are protected, restored and enhanced through coordinated efforts at international, national, regional and local levels guided by sound science and effective management. It is designed to increase the effectiveness of existing and new initiatives

North American Bird Conservation Initiative

The North American Bird Conservation Initiative helps protect the populations and habitats of North America's birds, including the whooping crane. Read more about this organization on its Web site.

Access this Web site from http://www.myreportlinks.com

and streams that crisscross the landscape, protecting the environment within a refuge remains a challenge.

Competing Demands for Water

The greatest challenge to wetland preservation, though, is finding enough water for all to use. The marshy environment of the Aransas National Wildlife Refuge is threatened because people are using so much of the water from the rivers that support it.

The wildlife habitat along the Platte River in Nebraska provides another example of too many demands on too little water. Farmers in Colorado, Wyoming, and Nebraska, who need water to irrigate their fields, compete with growing cities for the river's precious water. And environmentalists who want to preserve a portion of the Platte's natural habitat find themselves in conflict with both. Recently, the United States Bureau of Reclamation and the United States Fish and Wildlife Service worked with the three states to develop a plan to resolve the conflict. The plan involves storing water for environmental purposes, recharging aquifers near one of the Platte's tributaries, and regulating water used by Nebraska farmers who rely on wells. Aquifers are layers of earth, made up of rock, sand, or gravel, where water is found. Wells that drain aquifers near the river eventually lower the river's water level.

▶ **More Threats and Some Solutions**

Pollution in many forms threatens wading birds because polluted substances often end up in bodies of water. But oil and chemical spills pose a particular threat to whooping cranes. About three quarters of the country's wild whooping cranes spend their winters in a refuge on the Texas Gulf Coast. In the Gulf of Mexico and along an intracoastal canal, a serious oil or chemical spill is a real possibility. Efforts to prevent toxic spills continue to be made.

Another continuing threat to whooping cranes is the presence of power lines. Recently, however, some power lines have been tagged to make them more visible to the whoopers, and this effort seems to be paying off in fewer collisions.

The story of the whooping crane and the efforts to save this native North American species illustrates what

Humans have been the primary threat to whooping cranes. It is up to us to make sure that this majestic North American bird species survives.

people can do when they put their minds—and their imaginations—to work. It took an idea as simple and creative as disguising one's human form and holding a crane puppet for wildlife experts to succeed at raising wild whooping cranes. And it took two imaginative pilots, flying ultralight aircraft and wearing white costumes, to lead whoopers on an eastern migration route that the species had not followed for centuries. Thanks to people spending countless hours, a great deal of energy, and a lot of money, the whooping crane's recovery is an inspiring success story. How much better would it be, then, if we took action to preserve species and protect their habitats *before* both became endangered? Consider the words of John Sawhill, who was, among other things, the president of the Nature Conservancy, a leading environmental organization: "In the end, our society will be defined not only by what we create, but by what we refuse to destroy."[5]

In 1973, Congress took the farsighted step of creating the Endangered Species Act, widely regarded as the world's strongest and most effective wildlife conservation law. It set an ambitious goal: to reverse the alarming trend of human-caused extinction that threatened the ecosystems we all share.

Each book in this series explores the life of an endangered animal. The books tell how and why the animals have become endangered and explain the efforts being made to restore their populations.

The United States Fish and Wildlife Service and the National Marine Fisheries Service share responsibility for administration of the Endangered Species Act. Over time, animals are added to, reclassified in, or removed from the federal list of Endangered and Threatened Wildlife and Plants. At the time of publication, all the animals in this series were listed as endangered species. The most up-to-date list can be found at **http://www.fws.gov/endangered/wildlife.html#Species.**

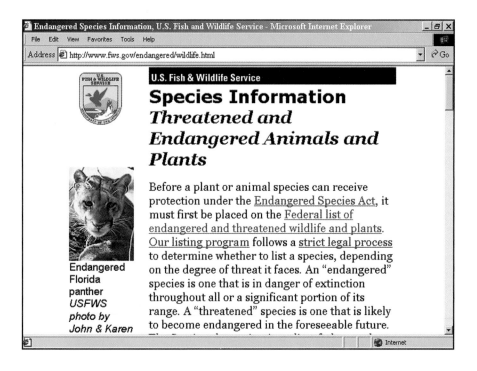

Report Links

The Internet sites described below can be accessed at
http://www.myreportlinks.com

▶**International Crane Foundation (ICF)**
Editor's Choice This conservation organization works to preserve the world's cranes.

▶**Whooping Crane Conservation Association**
Editor's Choice The WCCA was the first private organization to preserve whooping cranes.

▶**Operation Migration**
Editor's Choice Two men use ultralights to lead whooping cranes on a new migration.

▶**Whooping Crane Eastern Partnership**
Editor's Choice This partnership is making it possible for whooping cranes to survive.

▶**USGS Patuxent Wildlife Research Center**
Editor's Choice Visit this federal research lab and refuge that is helping to save whooping cranes.

▶**National Wildlife Federation: Whooping Crane**
Editor's Choice This site provides a comprehensive look at whoopers and efforts to save them.

▶**Alberta Sustainable Resource Development: Whooping Cranes**
The provincial government of Alberta, Canada, works to save whooping crane habitat.

▶**AMNH: Endangered!: Whooping Crane**
Learn about whooping cranes from this American Museum of Natural History Web site.

▶**Aransas National Wildlife Refuge**
Every winter, a flock of wild whooping cranes calls the Aransas National Wildlife Refuge home.

▶**Audubon: Whooping Crane**
The National Audubon Society Web site provides information on the tallest North American bird.

▶**Chassahowitzka National Wildlife Refuge**
The eastern migratory flock of whooping cranes makes its winter home in this wildlife refuge.

▶**Cornell Lab of Ornithology**
The Web site of Cornell University's Ornithology Laboratory provides information on birds.

▶**Critter Corner: Whooping Crane**
A fact sheet on whooping cranes is provided by this National Wildlife Refuge Association Web site.

▶**Defenders of Wildlife: On the Wing Again**
This wildlife conservation organization is committed to saving the whooping crane and other species.

▶**Environment Canada: Whooping Crane**
Environment Canada's Web site on whooping cranes offers information on this species at risk.

Report Links

The Internet sites described below can be accessed at
http://www.myreportlinks.com

▶**Fish and Wildlife Research Institute**
This site offers articles about whoopers and the efforts to establish flocks in Florida.

▶**Flight School**
Read about a human-led whooping crane migration.

▶**Hinterland: Bird Fact Sheets: Whooping Crane**
This Canadian Wildlife Federation fact sheet offers information on whooping cranes.

▶**Journey North: Whooping Crane**
At this site, read about the spring and fall migrations of the whooping crane.

▶**Natural Resources Foundation of Wisconsin**
The Natural Resources Foundation of Wisconsin is a partner in the fight to save whoopers.

▶**North American Bird Conservation Initiative**
At this site, learn about the NABCI's efforts to protect North American bird species.

▶**Platte River Whooping Crane Maintenance Trust, Inc.**
This nonprofit organization is dedicated to conserving the migratory bird habitat of the Platte.

▶**Roger Tory Peterson Institute of Natural History**
Visit the Web site of the Roger Tory Peterson Institute, dedicated to nature study.

▶**Rowe Sanctuary**
This Audubon sanctuary on Nebraska's Platte River is a migratory refuge for two crane species.

▶**Species at Risk: Whooping Crane**
This is the Canadian Wildlife Service species overview of the whooping crane.

▶**Theodore Roosevelt Association: Conservationist**
At this site, learn about Theodore Roosevelt's efforts to preserve American wildlife.

▶**USFWS Endangered Species Program: Kids Corner**
This USFWS Web site offers ways you can help save endangered species.

▶**Whoopers, Who's Your Momma?**
With the help of ultralight aircraft, whooping cranes learn to migrate.

▶**Whooping Crane: *Grus americana***
This site looks at efforts to establish whooping cranes at Yellowstone.

▶**Wood Buffalo National Park of Canada**
Wood Buffalo National Park is Canada's summer home for the whooping crane.

aquifer—A stratum, or layer, of earth in which water is found underground.

brood *(verb)*—The term used for the way birds use their body heat to keep their eggs or their chicks warm. Whooping cranes brood their eggs as they take turns sitting on the nest for a month. Mother whooping cranes brood their chicks by making a little tent with their wings.

clutch—All the eggs in a nest. Whooping cranes usually lay a clutch of two eggs.

cohort—A group of young whoopers that stays together for protection and companionship. Whooping cranes can begin to form cohorts about the time they learn to fly.

critical habitat—Definite land areas where animals need to live or range in order to survive.

ecosystem—All of the animals, plants, and other living things that make up a community in a certain environment.

fledge *(verb)*—The term used for growing real feathers and learning to fly. Whooping cranes fledge, or learn to fly, when they are between seventy and eighty days old.

forage *(verb)*—To move about, looking for food. Cranes forage by walking and pecking at what they see moving on the ground. They also peck at grains or berries from plants, and they use their bills to dig in the mud for crabs.

habitat—An area that supports animals and plants by providing them with what they need to survive, including food, water, shelter, and protection from predators. For example, a wetland habitat provides a whooping crane with food, vegetation for nests, and water for protection when it sleeps.

instinct—A behavior that is part of an animal from birth and that fulfills a vital need. Sometimes an instinct needs to be "triggered." Whooping cranes are born with an instinct to migrate, but they need to be taught the migration route.

migration—The flight between a summer nesting area and a winter feeding area. Migrating birds usually make this trip in the spring and the fall.

naturalist—A person who studies natural history, especially zoology and botany.

nonmigratory—Refers to cranes or other birds that live year-round in one area.

oxbow lake—A crescent-shaped lake that is formed when a winding part of a stream or river is cut off from its main channel.

primary feathers—The feathers on the outside edge of birds' wings. Also known as the primaries, these feathers can be spread and maneuvered to control speed and direction.

recovery plan—A plan developed by experts hired by the United States Fish and Wildlife Service that serves as a guide to help an endangered or threatened species recover, or increase in number.

sandhill crane—The other crane species native to North America. Sandhills are gray and smaller than whooping cranes. Their wingspan is six to seven feet. Like whooping cranes, sandhill cranes have red caps that change in color to reflect their mood. Unlike whooping cranes, sandhill cranes are not endangered.

thermal—A rising air current caused by warmer air from the earth's surface meeting the cooler air above it. Birds may use the lift of thermals to help them soar, or fly without beating their wings.

wetlands—Low-lying ecosystem where the water table is always at or near the surface. Water moves slowly or not at all in wetlands. Wetlands help to regulate the earth's water cycle. They also filter the water supply, prevent soil erosion, and absorb floodwaters.

wildlife refuge—Land set aside to promote the survival of wildlife by providing an appropriate habitat and protection from humans. Many refuges permit recreational activities, such as hiking and boating, as well as hunting and fishing in season. The United States Wildlife Refuge System protects more than 93 million acres. Private individuals and societies (including the Nature Conservancy and the National Audubon Society) also establish wildlife refuges.

Chapter 1. A History-Making Flight

1. Operation Migration Field Journals, Joseph Duff, *In the Field,* November 3, 2001, <http://www.operationmigration.org/Field_Journal.html> (March 15, 2005).

2. United States Department of the Interior, United States Fish and Wildlife Service, "Endangered and Threatened Wildlife and Plants; Establishment of a Nonessential Experimental Population of Whooping Cranes in the Eastern United States," *Federal Register,* June 26, 2001, vol. 66, no. 123, p. 33904.

3. Ibid.

4. Paul A. Johnsgard, *Cranes of the World* (Bloomington: Indiana University Press, 1983), p. 188.

5. Whooping Crane Eastern Partnership, "Just Ahead of the Ultralight-led Cranes, Wild Whooping Crane Completes Fall Migration," November 22, 2004, <http://www.bringbackthecranes.org/media/2004/nr-112204.htm> (February 11, 2005).

Chapter 2. Whooping Cranes in the Wild

1. Environment Canada, "Quenching the Peace-Athabasca Delta," Science and the Environment Bulletin, September 1999, <http://www.ec.gc.ca/science/sandesept99/article4_e.html> (January 3, 2005).

2. Paul A. Johnsgard, *Cranes of the World* (Bloomington: Indiana University Press, 1983), p. 193.

3. Scott R. Swengel, George W. Archibald, David H. Ellis, and Dwight G. Smith, "Behavior Management" in David H. Ellis, George F. Gee, and Claire M. Mirande, eds., *Cranes: Their Biology, Husbandry, and Conservation* (U.S. Department of the Interior, National Biological Service, Washington, D.C., and International Crane Foundation, Baraboo, Wis., 1996), p. 106.

4. Ibid., p.107.

5. Marianne Wellington, Ann Burke, Jane M. Nicolich,

and Kathleen O'Malley, "Chick Rearing," in David H. Ellis, George F. Gee, and Claire M. Mirande, eds., *Cranes: Their Biology, Husbandry, and Conservation* (U.S. Department of the Interior, National Biological Service, Washington, D.C., and International Crane Foundation, Baraboo, Wis., 1996), pp. 79–80.

6. Peter Matthiessen, *The Birds of Heaven: Travels With Cranes* (New York: North Point Press, 2001), p. 293.

7. Johnsgard, p. 11.

8. Ibid., p. 12.

9. Ibid., p. 27.

10. *Grus Americana* Newsletter, Newsletter Excerpts, "Record Numbers of Whoopers Migrating to Aransas, Texas," September 2003, p. 2, <http://www.whoopingcrane .com/Newsletter_2003_fall.htm> (November 1, 2004).

11. Johnsgard, p. 25.

12. Swengel et al., p. 114.

13. Ibid., p. 115.

Chapter 3. Threats to Survival

1. David Rains Wallace, *Life in the Balance* (New York: Harcourt Brace Jovanovich, Publishers, 1987), p. 208.

2. Ibid., p. 210.

3. Ibid.

4. Ibid., p. 216.

5. Annenberg/CPB, *Learner.org,* "Journey North: The Bald Eagle—DDT," n.d., <http://www.learner.org/jnorth/ tm/DDT.html> (April 14, 2005).

6. Wallace, p. 216.

7. *Grus Americana* Newsletter, Newsletter Excerpts, "San Marcos River Foundation Continues Struggle to Protect Whooping Crane Habitat," September 2003, p. 6, <http://www.whoopingcrane.com/Newsletter_2003_fall .htm> (November 1, 2004).

8. Les Line, "Bringing the Magic Back to the Platte," *National Wildlife* magazine, April/May 2000, vol. 38, no. 3, p. 3, <http://www.nwf.org/national wildlife/article.cfm? issue ID=29&article ID=694> (February 7, 2005).

9. Ibid.

10. Environment Canada, "Quenching the Peace-Athabasca Delta," *Science and the Environment Bulletin,* September 1999, <http://www.ec.gc.ca/science/ sandesept99/article4_e.html> (January 3, 2005).

11. National Wildlife Federation Web site, "Whooping Crane," n.d., <http//www.nwf.org/wildlife/whoopingcrane> (March 15, 2005).

Chapter 4. Protection

1. Clifford J. Sherry, *Endangered Species* (Santa Barbara, Calif.: ABC-CLIO, Inc., 1998), p. 9.

2. Eric Jay Dolin, *Smithsonian Book of Wildlife Refuges* (Washington, D.C.: Smithsonian Institution Press, 2003), p. 10.

3. Ibid., p. 1.

4. Doug Stewart et al, "How Conservation Grew From a Whisper to a Roar," *National Wildlife* magazine, December/January 2000, vol. 38, no. 1, p. 3, <http:// www.nwf.org/nationalwildlife/article.cfm?articleid= 241&issueid=27> (January 25, 2005).

5. Ibid., p. 8.

6. Jeff Curtis and Bob Davison, "The Endangered Species Act: Thirty Years on the Ark," *Open Spaces Quarterly,* October 5, 2004, p. 1, <http://www.open-spaces.com/ article-v5n3-davison.php> (March 15, 2005).

7. Ibid., p. 7.

8. Curtis and Davison, p. 2.

9. The United States Fish and Wildlife Service Web site, "The Endangered Species Act of 1973," Section 3, no. 18, <http://endangered.fws.gov/esa.html> (March 17, 2005).

10. Curtis and Davison, p. 6.

Chapter 5. Saving the Whooping Crane

1. Peter Matthiessen, *The Birds of Heaven: Travels With Cranes* (New York: North Point Press, 2001), p. 280.

2. United States Department of the Interior, United States Fish and Wildlife Service, "Endangered and Threatened Wildlife and Plants; Establishment of a Nonessential Experimental Population of Whooping Cranes in the Eastern United States," *Federal Register,* June 26, 2001, vol. 66, no. 123, p. 33903.

3. Ibid., p. 33904.

4. Matthiessen, p. 281.

5. Ibid., p. 284.

6. Ibid., p. 298.

7. Operation Migration Web site, "Operation Migration: Our Work in 1993," <http://www.operationmigration.org/work_1993.html> (April 11, 2005).

8. Operation Migration, Field Journals, Joseph Duff, *In the Field,* Nov. 5, 2001, <http://www.operationmigration.org/Field_Journal.html> (March 15, 2005).

Chapter 6. Raising Wild Whooping Cranes

1. United States Geological Survey, Patuxent Wildlife Research Center, "Whooping Crane Hatching Countdown," <http://whoopers.usgs.gov/coolfacts.htm> (March 15, 2005).

2. Marianne Wellington, Ann Burke, Jane M. Nicolich, and Kathleen O'Malley, "Chick Rearing" in David H. Ellis, George F. Gee, and Claire M. Mirande, eds., *Cranes: Their Biology, Husbandry, and Conservation* (U.S. Department of the Interior, National Biological Service, Washington, D.C., and International Crane Foundation, Baraboo, Wis., 1996), p. 78.

3. Ibid., p. 92.

4. Ibid., p. 78.

5. Ibid., p. 88.

6. Ibid.

7. Ibid., p. 89.

8. USGS, Patuxent Wildlife Research Center, "Whooping Crane Hatching Countdown," n.d., <http://whoopers.usgs .gov/coolfacts.htm> (February 11, 2005).

Chapter 7. The Future of Whooping Cranes

1. Whooping Crane Eastern Partnership, "Just Ahead of the Ultralight-led Cranes, Wild Whooping Crane Completes Fall Migration," November 22, 2004, <http://www .bringbackthecranes.org/media/2004/nr-112204.htm> (February 11, 2005).

2. *Grus Americana* Newsletter, Newsletter Excerpts, "Hosting an Ageless Journey," September 2003, p. 14, <http://www.whoopingcrane.com/Newsletter_2003_fall .htm> (November 1, 2004).

3. David Rains Wallace, *Life in the Balance* (New York: Harcourt Brace Jovanovich, Publishers, 1987), p. 219.

4. Ibid., p. 220.

5. John Sawhill, The Nature Conservancy, as quoted in the Web site of the *National Wildlife Federation,* "Wildlife Quotes," n.d., <http://www.nwf.org/wildlife/quote/> (August 1, 2005).

Bright, Michael. *Animals of the Rivers, Lakes, and Wetlands.* Brookfield, Conn.: Copper Beech Books, 2002.

Craats, Rennay. *Whooping Cranes.* Minneapolis: Lake Street Publishers, 2003.

Duden, Jane. *Whoop Dreams: The Historic Migration.* Des Moines: Perfection Learning Corporation, 2004.

Dudley, Karen. *Whooping Cranes.* Austin, Tex.: Raintree Steck-Vaughn, 1997.

DuTemple, Lesley A. *North American Cranes.* Minneapolis: Carolrhoda Books, 1999.

Greive, Bradley Trevor. *Priceless: The Vanishing Beauty of a Fragile Planet.* Kansas City, Mo.: Andrews McMeel Publishers, 2003.

Lasky, Kathryn. *She's Wearing a Dead Bird on Her Head.* New York: Hyperion, 1995.

Lerner, Carol. *On the Wing: American Birds in Migration.* New York: HarperCollins Publishers, 2001.

Salmansohn, Pete, and Stephen W. Kress. *Saving Birds: Heroes Around the World.* Gardiner, Maine: Tilbury House, 2003.

Sayre, April Pulley. *Endangered Birds of North America.* New York: Twenty-First Century Books, 1997.

Somervill, Barbara A. *Animal Survivors of the Wetlands.* New York: Franklin Watts, 2004.